VAHNI CAPILDEO is a Trinidadian Scottish writer inspired by other voices, ranging from live Caribbean connexions and an Indian diaspora background to the landscapes where Capildeo travels and lives. Capildeo's poetry (seven books and four pamphlets) includes *Measures of Expatriation*, awarded the Forward Prize for Best Collection in 2016. Following a DPhil in Old Norse literature, Capildeo has worked in academia; in culture for development, with Commonwealth Writers; and as an Oxford English Dictionary lexicographer. *Skin Can Hold* reflects on experiments with masquerade and embodiment undertaken during Capildeo's Judith E. Wilson Poetry Fellowship and Harper-Wood Studentship at Cambridge, and completed thanks to a Douglas Caster Cultural Fellowship at the University of Leeds.

T0159811

VAHNI CAPILDEO

Skin Can Hold

CARCANET

First published in Great Britain in 2019 by
Carcanet
Alliance House, 30 Cross Street
Manchester M2 7AQ
www.carcanet.co.uk

Cover image: 'Battle of Flowers, Baranquilla Carnaval'
© Kike Calvo / Alamy 2019

A CIP catalogue record for this book is
available from the British Library.
ISBN 978 1 78410 731 4

Book design by Andrew Latimer
Printed in Great Britain by SRP Ltd, Exeter, Devon

MIX
Paper from
responsible sources
FSC® C014540

The publisher acknowledges financial
assistance from Arts Council England.

Supported using public funding by
ARTS COUNCIL
ENGLAND

Contents

Who comes walking in the dark night time?
Whose boot of steel tramps down the slender grass?
It is the man of death, my love, the strange invader
watching you sleep and aiming at your dream.

Martin Carter, 'This Is the Dark Time My Love'
Poems of Resistance from British Guiana (1954) [1953]

i.m.

DR WINSTON MCGARLAND BAILEY

1941–2018

Master Calypsonian, 'The Shadow'

SKIN CAN HOLD

I
PROLOGUE

THE BROWN BAG SERVICE

We would like to show our appreciation. We would like to show our appreciation to all our customers travelling today. We would like to show our appreciation to all our customers travelling today on the brown bag service.

Customers are courteously requested to courteously request brown bags in Wholemeal, Bleachers, or Cricket sizes. Wholemeal, Bleachers and Cricket are new sizes tailored to your citizenship incorporation experience and your journey with us today. If you have failed to place a timely sizing request on the brown bag service, a standard-issue brown bag will personally have been issued to you personally. We accept no liability for the issue of Wholemeal, Bleachers and Cricket sizes. Customers are courteously reminded that no other sizing system worldwide or from the origin of recorded time corresponds to the sizing system on the brown bag service. Make your choice with uprightness and care.

In exceptional and normal circumstances, customers may be deemed to require a cranial refitting. The cranial refitting facilities are currently closed. We aim to deliver a fully anachronistic incorporation experience on the brown bag service.

Customers travelling with children must ensure that every child travelling on the brown bag service is individually brown-bagged. Children are expected to be covered to up to 66.67% in this citizenship incorporation experience, and to perform their toilet functions with reasonable effectiveness and without removal of the brown bag.

Customers allegedly or certifiedly afflicted with conditions such as claustrophobia, breathing difficulties, body dysmorphia, conversationalism, appetite, vulnerability, mascara, hope, or being long in the tooth, must disembark the vehicle and return the brown bag to the nearest collection point, after which they will be reassessed and Wholemeal, Bleachers, or Cricket will be reassigned.

The doors are now shut.

Customers, cover your faces.

Attendants are already in the carriages, performing the necessary checks.

Please comply with the attendants, to maximise your enjoyment. You may be selected for the scissors service; this is optional, but once again you are invited to comply.

We look forward to your feedback on the other side.

(IN THE)

Z I O AM O

(LEFT)

THE

C
I
R
C
U
S

II
BLACKBOX CLEANOUT

FOUR ABLUTIONS

Texts to be included and/or discarded by performers preparing for actions

I

Standing at a great height in a black box rigged by chaos, take a stainless steel tankard. Dip it into the white washing-up bowl. You are not nude. Your hanging sleeves will get wet. You have to stoop. The white washing-up bowl is at your feet on the platform which was described as secure and is unstable. Your core and sacrum will find the necessary elegance. Balance is necessary, elegant. Pour, now, the contents of the stainless steel tankard (you could store your breast in it, if you were St Agatha (you are not nude)) over the edge. Below is another platform, also unstable, also secure. Pour into the middling-sized glass bowl. The water that you pour is full of flowers. You dip and orange ixora, yellow carnations, scarlet and white rose petals make the water thick and alarming. This is as sweet as blood. Clear on that. Limbed, glistening, repeated.

II

Lying blindfolded on the floor in a black box rigged by chaos, you are motionless at his feet. Motionless means breathing. You are not dead. You may be nude, or painted; underworn, or unitarded; clothed in some way as if sewn into your skin, or as if skin is sewn on, and as if then freshly unclothed from your skin, meaning born rather than flayed, skinned of your clothes (but this will be supposed to have happened before (you just lie there)), you are ignored by him and knowable to any others as vulnerability in situ, a heap of lines that cannot be crossed out, except deletion by delivery is what his voice does. He reads in a beautiful voice. The evil in the room wants it petty, sieved, meshed, strained, howled: the voice surrounded by surrogate sound, the rustle of unhung shutters. But it is a beautiful voice. He does not notice you. He does not look down. He steps over you; over and around. He pours sand over you, without looking. He wets the sand with plain water from his travelling cup. He pats down the sand. This is your body.

III

Raising your right hand in the air in a black box rigged by chaos, you raise a long-stemmed iris into the air. Yellow river irises are called flags. This one is purple. Staying an iris-length away, outline the man. Iris-length varies according to how you fold your arm and where you hold the stalk. Whipped and immaculate, the giant reader is tied to his microphone with shredded clingfilm, the dolphin-choking image of liaisons past. There is wet sand along the ground beside him. There is a disaccordioned platform and spillage of water and flowers behind him. He reads with the abstraction of a bichon frisé abandoned in the Hofgarten. You stoop, stretch, circle, segment, re-attach the relation of your body to the space around him. The iris is painterly. It brushes him into existence. The long Chinese scroll of himself acquires a mountain of characters. Is this a ritual of freeing or a ritual of realisation? In an alternative version of this performance, there were only two audience members. All the black plastic chairs facing the reader were empty. One audience member stood behind the reader's right shoulder, in shadow, revolving slowly on the spot. The other stood at an angle to the reader's left shoulder: a mannequin with a blonde wig placed on the neck, and no face. In the original version, there is no revolution and no pre-execution. There is sand, water, metal, glass and petals. The black plastic chairs may or may not be full. The task is to notice whether the rhythm of the outlining iris's touch and the voice with its beautiful cadence form together a thing too harmonious for a black box: the conjuration of a field; conjuration on which a door can be shut, or opened.

IV

Shaken from the upper balcony of the black box building, metre after metre of blue, green, bluegreen, azure cloth: water to the terracotta cladding. This building has known such thirsts. The arms shaking the cloth appear healthily feathered. Standing on a ledge under a tree, a thin girl sings vowels. Her arms are raised. She is rigged with makeshift wings that double as racks for scarlet and yellow ribbons: wishes and blessings blank of desire, since nobody but herself tied them on. No performance, such as untying ribbons to give to passersby, is involved. Clear about that, she and the tree stand and sing. It is their marriage. They have inherited the building – a ledge.

SWEET FOOL

He has gone out upon the waters
against advice; sure of nothing but that
he must go, he has gone. Out upon
waters that count for nothing: profit
nor holiday. The waters clean him
cleanly him as he was shareable
darkness, but for that one night found sitting
kinglike, too blacked-out to sing; his drinkers
his court, his courted home kicking him out;
the stickiness of people who used him
wiring and smearing his hair; his kisses
tighter than reconnexions, tightened
like the fingers of an uncollected
child. A child he has gone out. The waters
bob and sunrise is a spinning top.
He has done everything, hung his shirt out
cleanly, clean blue and white stripes on the line.

SHAME

The performer wears a coat of mirrors. A Venetian wire mask covers her face. Glow in the dark paint, white and pale violet, covers the skin of her face. Long black velvet gloves cover her arms. The long black velvet gloves extend into the sleeves of the mirrored coat. The performer carries a cloth bag. A lucky dip! Now and then she goes among the audience, inviting them to dip their hands into the cloth bag. What luck. An Empire biscuit. What luck. An apple dedicated to Morgan le Fay. What luck. A sanitary towel with the names of goddesses inked onto it: red Ceres, crimson Persephone, bloody Artemis, scarlet Aphrodite...

Who is not here?

Why are they not here?

Where are they?

I have no shame but fury

I have no shame but weariness

I have no shame but a sense of enclosure

I have no shame but a sense of déjà vu

I have no shame but the knowledge I shall be disbelieved

I have no shame

I am ashamed

I am not ashamed of

I am ashamed for

Shame on behalf of others is ageing

Shame on behalf of others is distancing

Shame on behalf of others is translating

Shame is not in my body except as a spur to action

I would like to tell you a story. A few stories.

Where are my friends? I have friends in this city. Where are my friends?

What made this week unlike all other weeks?

Do not SHE me

'You need someone from your own culture,' he said.
'What culture is that?' I asked.
'Trinidadian,' he said, monotheistically.

I am unshakably surrounded by numerous dead and therefore
it is almost impossible to shame me. To grow up in an ancient
polytheism is to have fed the dead with balls of black sesame seed;
to have your secret name called in front of the fire in the line of
the names of your dead; and to see them in your sleep, drumming
and swaying, drumming and swaying, the night before one of
your ordeals, which you survive. Your ordeals were not meant to
occur. Your ordeals are not part of it; they wash away; you pass
on. You? No, not you. I. Self-censorship is not shame. I have not
been religion-shamed by the fascists who these years have been
carving symbols into living foreheads and slaughter people who
are preparing their meals. Not to speak is a form of speaking.

When was I ashamed?

I was not ashamed as an infant when he sat me on his chest, my
chunky little legs wide and my cottony vulva unconscious of being
close to his face; nor when he made me learn to tweak his nipples
until they were peaks, though I felt responsible for his pain, and
sorry for him when pleasurably he wanted it harder and harder. His
penis was further from me than my torso was long. I was that small.
I was not ashamed when he folded his underpants down and held
the rubber hose quiet with one hand while asking me to brush his
hair flat. I felt responsible for how his hair looked, and sorry for the
pubic area, which did not suit being brushed flat. I felt responsible
and sorry, as if I had power. From feeling as if I had power, I have
not lost power. I did not have shame. Now I exercise power.

I was not ashamed when he told me that the red brick dust that
sifted over the walkway next to the house was 'plip' and that
plip meant shit. He told me that the plip came from my doll. He
took my doll and did not have to take her forcibly. I had been
informed that he was interesting, a gifted individual. He took my
doll and placed her face down. He moved her up and down like
a scrubbing brush, making her eat plip. She took her punishment
mutely and I did not reinvent her voice. I observed his actions,
and the disgust on his face. He hated the body of the doll, bodily,
and in her he hated me bodily. I was curious. I was curious but
the curiosity overcame the responsibility to protect. The curiosity
overcame the urge to possess. Now I have curiosity, and power,
and still do not have shame.

I was ashamed when I broke the egg. There was a tree with fruits
like miniature apples. The flesh of these fruits, when ripe, tasted
faintly rotten. The canopy of the tree spread like many arms
with many eyes and many mouths, like a Leroy Clarke carnival
costume. Each branch of the tree, down to the smallest twig,
was netted with thorns. The whole tree swayed, the net of a net.

Caught up in the tree were many dead and dying birds, also the unhatched cocoons of giant moths and monarch butterflies, like the souls in a carnival maker's hereafter. Some birds would try to nest in the tree. From one of these nests, a few thick-shelled eggs had tipped out on to the semi-concrete floor of the garden. One had not broken. In front of him I took a doll, a wooden doll the size of a thumb, like the souls in between incarnations. I pretended to be playing aeroplanes and threw it to hit the egg. What had been dead but not smashed now smashed and the yolk that would have come to life as flight glopped out. He observed my actions, and there was disgust in his voice. *Why did I do that?* I was ashamed for I did not hate the egg, or the doll, or my body, but I had outraged all three of us bodily, for we were in the image and likeness of one another. The occurrence of the pretence as play; the occurrence of protest as pretend play; the performance of self-harm as protest: with its roots in the shade of the netted tree, this was shame.

When was I ashamed?

I was ashamed for my friend and colleague Athena who sent me an email about a thousand words long when I left the online angloamerican feminist group 'protoform', which had been expressing pity for our Irish sisters and hunting down its own members verbally, as one rule of protoform is not to talk about protoform. I was ashamed for how Athena had received the (privately communicated) story of someone who had been looked at with disgust by her beautician. 'Use *at least* two of these,' said the beautician, handing over two intimate wipes. We were told how the beautician winced with disgust while carrying out the intimate wax. She made faces each time she applied and removed the strips. We were told how the person lying down could feel the rosy fingertips wincing away on contact with the brown skin, then returning with unkindness to rip, while the eyes half closed and would not check. Wince. Rip. No check. The skin was stripped and festered and purpled and scarred. The ancient and worshipful triangle of mystery became the record of an intimate war. 'That's interpellation, right?!' Athena exclaimed to me. But no. I was feeling it in my own brown skin. I had no words. Silence was purple. I had no words when Athena shared a story not hers to share, of a friend whose mandoctor jokingly asked if her boyfriend had any photographs of the area he himself needed to check medically. Shame on behalf of others is wearying. No, Athena, I did not say and did not want to say. Your friend was being seen as a woman, a sex-object, yes, but not isolated; she was understood in relation to a desirous male. Your friend was still a type of human. In the other case there was only one woman. The beautician. One woman being forced to touch nasty *stuff*. She hurt and marked another woman because the other woman, being a different colour, was perceived only as nasty *stuff*. Shame on behalf of others is tiring. I hold it in the bowl of my pelvis, as empty as a night of timed-out stars. Shame on behalf of others flips into fury. I do not have a good word for my friend Athena. I do not have a good face to show my friend Athena. Nor are these words bad. They are what were.

I was not ashamed when the powerful editor-poet-translator Heinrich asked to meet me in a café, ostensibly to discuss the manuscript of my second book, but really to tell me to stop writing. Who read my poetry? Friends and family? Why did I use epigraphs? My book was antipoetic and destructive of poetry. He had shown it to his friend Thea and it had made her feel stupid. Thea was not a stupid woman, but my book had made her feel stupid. It was an unpleasant experience for the reader. Did I know that people used to write like that in antiquity but they don't write like that any more? Nobody would publish it. I should not try to get it published. He was a very busy man. He was ill. He had flu. He was doing me a favour by agreeing to meet me and tell me the truth. He bet I wished now that I had ordered something stronger to drink than water. I was not ashamed of my book or of my being, though in demeaning the one he was meaning the other. I was ashamed for the kind astronomer who had introduced this man to me. Besides, I had new dead surrounding me. As the powerful editor-poet-translator Heinrich got up to leave, he put his hand out and slithered towards him the copy of my first book which I had given him as a courtesy at the start of our meeting. After denouncing my poetry and attempting to put a stop to it, he was about to go away with a gift copy of my first book in his bag. I knew he would eat it. But I had new dead surrounding me. Two tall women. I felt them; I almost saw them, like a gleam and swiftness of Anna-Karenina-trainspeed in my peripheral vision. They were distinctly Sylvia Plath and Virginia Woolf. They knew they were dead. They knew how they had died. And they were hella angry. I could not let him get away. I could not let him get away with having killed them. For he was surrounded by the living: the self-immortalising men, who immortalise each other, having immolated women. I stood up too. Suddenly tall. That made three of us, and none of him. 'Give me my book back please.' All one phrase. No comma. My voice was sharp and he looked carved up. Shame was somewhere in the room. Shame almost had transferred on to him. Lord have mercy, shame was none of I; but I knew I had been blocked, and would be blocked again, by one of the good guys.

I was not ashamed when I had to deliver the creative writing syllabus that someone else had written. I was not ashamed when, as a visiting lecturer, I had been issued with no keys or staff card, and was followed by the security guard through corridors and up three flights of eighteenth-century stairs. I was not ashamed when none of my salaried and contracted colleagues who had promised to be in the office to let in the visiting lecturers had bothered to be in, and I could not access or prove access to the office. I was not ashamed when I had to teach my students sitting in the corridor, our backs to the wall, mid-morning alcohol on their breath. I was furious. I was not ashamed for the white feminist colleague whose sterling vulnerability meant that she could not face being at a particular place, once a week, to let in a whatever to do whatever with whatever. I was not ashamed. I had been brought up with caste privilege, and I had the illusion of being in control, and therefore able to make things right by some unminuted process of transformation. The tutorials on the floor would be the best tutorials. The reading lists would be in order and the in-line editing would be inked in by my own hand. I was ashamed in class when I had to deliver the creative writing syllabus that someone else had written, and to ask my students to contemplate their 'worst memory'. One of the keenest students tried, and left in distress, her high auburn hair as if on fire; the one who turned up had been forced out. I had been brought up with caste privilege, and I had the illusion of being in control, and therefore able to make things right, and to be responsible. Shame on behalf of others flips into fury. It is with the fury of that shame that I should have refused; that I can refuse. I re-fuse.

Creative writing exercise.

What does shame look like? Sound like? Feel like? Smell like? Taste like?

What colour is shame?

Shamelessness. I can do shamelessness.

Eyes without melanin, self-righteous eyes, crystal with crying tears of self-righteous anger; the eyes of structural racists at well-meaning gatherings. I have a story. I'm not ashamed. I'm not interested.

The voice that hurts and is heard. It nightingale-hurts, knowing its jewels will be heard. It says, 'He's a friend.' It says, 'She wanted. To do. Something good. For you.'

Shamelessness does not feel, smell, or taste until it is at home, its home, where you are not, you are not at home, where is your home, and you don't celebrate Christmas, do you? Shamelessness is polyfleece. I open this tap and drink it offcast in the water. Well.

You can do shamelessness. Shameless.

Touchstone:	[...] This is the very false gallop of verses: why do you infect yourself with them?
Rosalind:	Peace, you dull fool! I found them on a tree.
Touchstone:	Truly, the tree yields bad fruit.
Rosalind:	I'll graff it with you, and then I shall graff it with a medlar: then it will be the earliest fruit i' the country; for you'll be rotten ere you be half ripe, and that's the right virtue of the medlar.
Touchstone:	You have said; but whether wisely or no, let the forest judge.

As You Like It III.ii.

| Macbeth: | I have lived long enough: my way of life Is fall'n into the sear, the yellow leaf; |

Macbeth V.iii.

| Edmund: | Look, sir, I bleed. |

King Lear II.i.

| Shylock: | [...] Hath not a Jew eyes? hath not a Jew hands, organs, dimensions, senses, affections, passions? fed with the same food, hurt with the same weapons, subject to the same diseases, healed by the same means, warmed and cooled by the same winter and summer, as a Christian is? If you prick us, do we not bleed? |

if you tickle us, do we not laugh? if you poison
us, do we not die? and if you wrong us, shall we not
revenge?

The Merchant of Venice III.i.

*The reader, in a black hood attached to an oversize black tunic, barely
moves. Each of the reader's joints is articulated in isolation. The head
may tilt slightly. This has nothing to do with the fingers. Nothing to
do with the points of the feet. If the torso moves, the tunic contains
the movement. The reader stands stage left, at a lectern.*

*In between each of the five acts of reading, the Fool fools. He brings
his own stepladder into the library. The library is a theatre where
the Fool is physical. He abases himself in between the rolling stacks.
Gibberish and grommelo are interspersed with lyric remixing of
Shakespeare's dramatic speeches. And oh, how the Fool can sing.*

I. NIGHT

Night has fallen, only when he said so; crawled into your brainpan
like a scarab in a catalogue come to life seeking Egyptian heat. Since
my dust is his, no need to squat on the precious square of grave
to build a tower block on the yogically balanced fundament of
funding fun whereby the governments of burnished countries by the
shedding boatload can be persuaded into subsidising English touring
companies, never mind their indigenous dance and articulation
perfect like a cactus limb, that holds water. Not to throw shade
on Shakespeare's home. It's an art to read graffiti on the tower
block: know what marks gangland territory, what swirls in sinclair
weather of beautiful cult attention, reviewed with all the impact
of slow-dropping hipster sperm. At once invisible, televisual and
visored, who is it at sponsored festivals singing of migrants forgets

23

the emphasis, singing instead of My Grants? Comedy in new-purchased turquoise lycra, stage helicopters and appropriated drums can be enough to make dividable spectators rise to the illusion, catch the spirit and fall down in fits, needing their bodies tapped, tripped, trapped and blown into. Shakespeare. It is alive, you see, and inconveniently alive in little, like the carp you'd tickle in a petting pool. The fish, tricked into a singularity of feeling as if your fingerpadding touch is one long line of its own swimming, returns for stimulation and wears down its protective slime by nub and looping in the straightened pool. It is alive, you hear, and inconveniently alive in middle, like a worker down a mineshaft marbling the earth with hurtful spirals, in his final resting place pressed flatter than the smart screens of rentable delight in steampunk pockets and in disconnexion from his labouring. It is alive, you type, and inconveniently alive in quick vertical, like on social media once, where a set of honest and original poets said no white actor should presume to play Othello since his is the only part black actors can without ripping the expensive delicate illusion of good theatre. I took by the throat these angels of the house, and clicked unlike.

The Fool fools in the library.

II. BLOOD

Look, sir, I bleed.
You're asking, where's the villain? Look, I bleed.
When men bleed, they shouldn't.
Men bleed when they shouldn't.
There are too many women in this play,
all of an age to bleed; none bore children.
Lunar and silent, they have spread a field
of blood beneath the action. Dirt has skirts,
smooth roads rust, tiled surfaces tainted
with vinegar; nothing wipes nothing out,

nothing can be reached directly; nothing
that does not shed a lining, shudder, rubbish
the chance to make one clean sweet queen bee line.
Look, sir. The whole tree of myself blushes
for your attention, came into flowering,
and was cut down; flowered again, cut down
again, not by a blade or breeze; the natural
result of inattention. Yours. The sea
breaks its allotted surface and self-harms,
changing where it goes, what can live inside it.
You'll buy me a new shirt. Hire people
to wipe up after me. I want their job:
want my blood on my hands, and in your eyes.

The Fool fools up and down the shelves, fooling even unto death.

III. THE EVENT

A: 'actions, no consequence'

                              don't change
                              direction, because
                              any second

take out: night
erayse: dark
scratch: still
put a line through: moon
remove: leaf

                                        now

take out: nerves
erayse: damage
scratch: solitude

put a line through: marvellous

                              dance!

take out: numerals
erayse: deities
scratch: cuneiform
put a line through: meaning
remove: mesopotamia

                              you

take out: naked
erayse: dazzle
scratch: soft
put a line through: my
remove: love

                              have it –
                              well done!
                              same difference!

Q: 'out of time'

The Fool takes an equal part in the dialogue. This is not
transcribed. It is a vibration persisting in the too-much-of-glass
building, part of the ephemeral archive. Fool and reader sing,
creature to creature.

IV. TREES

You're indecipherable like a tree, and treelike you proliferate your
gestures. I have thee not; I never see thee still. Still, so; furled,
limber, Pongerous; a lily of bread, peascod of the valley, medlar
of the fields, half a loaf of dafffodils, innocent violets. Advance
the pleachèd labyrinth of thine ear and let me clean it! *How much
wood would a woodchuck* – My father was a proper gentleman;
he opened doors for ladies, taught me alphabets and how to pitch
marbles. When he died they wound his shroud tying his head
off like an onion. Proceeding by outgrowing, *Le ver vert* – the
tree is a poem from somewhere buried. *– chuck if a woodchuck
could chuck wood?* Last May I saw his spirit, glad to walk the
day. He pointed me towards the cedar cabinets which yielded
luminous eggs, like mothballs, plasma and the planning stage of
innovations; some with elbows or coronet-shaped. *– va vers* –
Shakespeare burial instructions: sad cypress for the lovelorn; *If a
woodchuck could chuck* – alternatively, *– le verre vert* – willow;
best of all a birdcage. We'd be perched out on a limb, parched
like rice in sunshine, being feed and twitterers in one. Colleagues
on lunchbreak should know better than to shatter each other's
illusions. The one who told me dinosaurs had feathers and that
perchance Tyrannosaurus preyed and clucked like a free-range
Norfolk turkey; no matter. The best of all a birdcage, *– wood,*
what's beyond, so fool of song, bitter and sweet, military-issue
gloves, immortelle longings. My colleague ruin'd the choirs where
now agave syrup dinosaurs sing. Beyond *– then a woodchuck* It
was the nightosaur, no dawnosaur, that pierced the fearful hollow
of thine ear. Nightly she sings on yon pomegranate tree. Believe
me, love, it was the nightosaur. *– would chuck as much wood, as a
wood* – Unfold *– chuck* – a gentle and a bendable cave COULD.

*Fooling stops here. At the lectern, the reader in the black hood
falls silent. The City is forbidden to be performed.*

Shylock:	Hath…
Person A:	It is much too hot for June.
Shylock:	Hath not…
Person B:	When are you having your holiday?
Shylock:	Hath not a…
Person A:	I was booked for Sharm Al Sheikh. I love the sea. They've ruined it.
Person B:	You were looking forward…
Person A:	Now I'm afraid to fly.
Person B:	…to that.
Shylock:	Hath not a…
Person B:	It's the man with the gold chain again.
Shylock:	Eyes! Hands! Organs!
Person A:	Ignore him.
Shylock:	Dimensions! Senses!
Person B:	I can't understand what he's saying, can you?
Person A:	Afraid so.
Shylock:	Affections!
Person A:	He has a lovely house. Why he chooses to wander about the street…
Shylock:	Passions!
Person A:	…winter and summer…
Person B:	You're very good. I can't make out a word.
Shylock:	Bleed!

A NATIONAL LITERATURE

Poltergeist in the flat of the page,
s/he may be laughing & crying
as they write this.
You have no means of knowing.
Their oily fingers
burn like wicks; what they wear is white;
cloud conditions
appear sewn & sown; grey aircraft
could be stitching
your sampler house to the sky
you have no means
of knowing.
       You have been sticking
postage stamps to trees;
would that go somewhere if you could
wait – your cult is
the messenger as message; you
hope to interest
the forest in a system of rebuke,
as they write this
in rooms where corners resemble
handbells; emulsion
came out of tins like mid-air milk,
staying hanging
till you notice between the lines
someone weeping,
weeping & being beaten;
there is always,
even between the lines that speak
of breaks & brakes,

always someone
else who was present in writing –
when you thought you
knew – who you thought you were reading –
no means – in the garden singing

READING FOR COMPASS: RESPONSE TO MARK FORD, *ENTER, FLEEING*

Who was already there
when they entered fleeing?
Mélisande or Ariel
high on a swaying lamp
level with the poorest
ticket-purchasers, the gods?
It is a stage, and so
it is a stage. Silent,
the dreadlocked sound guy; drunk,
the artichoke-livered
lighting engineer. (Fair
fleeing, said the girl
milling through chilly days
in 50s Lancashire.)
Please. Respect the prologue.
Breathe. Engage deeper
than your artesian core.
Mr Ford has given
the curtain-opening
citation to a man
who exited fleeing:
the philosopher, Walter Benjamin.

Oh boy, the ghost of the loss of control
handles the red coins of language so well,
there's always a song coming on, a song
or a uniform. I know you are from
somewhere hot, too, where news flows sideways, pain
flowers from things with feathers, *white with fury*
someone older takes the centre stage; so
every poem contains a child, noises

of molestation off, power lines sour
as dough, dismissive as sphinxes, *flooded
with adrenaline*. Each normality
caps another normality, leaving
the Poet birdbrained hitchcock-style, h- h-
huh hit Hitchcock-style. Love's an enigma
like murder. Directions arrive as if
translated from the more helpful souls
in Dante's hell. Lime trees weep blood, money,
aromantic music. I blink. I drift.

Mr Ford's interlude
is Emily's; Nelly's
words, heavy as apples
to be stored, not painted;
there's nought outwith the text,
but I'm in Yorkshire, so
I know the thorn's embrace
by two honeysuckles,
and how the wife's angel
is the husband's ploughboy,
and that return's its own
ruinous reward. LOL.
'Lord O Lord'. Mickey Finn's
awake in time to change
shape, gecko in a wall-zone.
Trains chug between dark and
booked. Everyone's reading
something, stolen, anxious
in simultaneous reincarnation, fu-
ture always already
suture. Mr Ford gave,
or took, just one Brontë

line, which thins, wuthering,
into soul-fusion, poems
and epigraph cleaving.

Panting, ending, burning, invading, weeping,
burning, caressing, longing! Reworking
thickens the trunk of the text; avid O-
vid, vidi, video. The narrator
moors like a Heathcliff, thisport, anyport.
There's no contradiction between Bahrain
and D.H. Lawrence. It's raining skateboards
in the saintly desert of the Doppler-
effect brain. I misread 'left' as 'lift'. Gears
enter screeching. Breathe. In a box. All change.
I feel adrift in 'Adrift', where the frauds
claim exotic identities and needs.
Reading this returns me to my body.
Ruinous reward. Something as little
as a crab, *constrained* as *lungs*,
brings me back to poetry, *a problem*
that won't go away. Mr Ford didn't
get around to my corner of the world,
but still. He's been. Silverfishing. Reeling
and writhing through the censored, holy cheese,
paper landscapes, indelible ink seas.

Zaf, at breakfast we outfaced a peacock:
taxidermied, in the poetry hotel,
it ascended a red drape; a model head
looked on. And you supported Liverpool,
I Real Madrid, in the Brexit pub
where you, a man, were scowled at; I, female-
presenting, ushered into the garden
with the smoking couples and the big screen:
another typical poetry night.
You made up the StAnza number in March
when we jumped into the Scottish sea, cold
initiators of a new tradition.
All this to declare an interest: I know
your voice, speaking around events, reading
at your events, before I read your book;
more than I've read your book, which I've re-read.
This isn't what I'm used to. I grew up
as an inventor of voices for dead
books, impossible, inherited, odd
volumes, middle slices missing, made up;
colonial texts for memorisation
autoexecuted in rolling tones;
'Indo-European' languages drunk
like milk alchemised from blood, acquired
history. I know in my bones a desert,
or somesuch suddenly green lush place, where
our ancestors could have met with opposed
weaponry. What has survived of this is
us. And your advice: take heed of the vowels.

In each of these poems, *I* am with *you*.
They are with *us*. Clearly, you are careful
of the reader of these poems; and I
am a reader; alongside many more
who will stand with you in the post office,
on the cricket pitch, tumble down the hill
in forced fighting, wonder at poppies, hear
the *I* of *you* speaking to other *you*s:
working, buried, gone, separated, loved,
born, remembered, travelling, Rumi, Donne,
Jane Austen, Jabir; the parted *lyric eye*
you share with Shakespeare through reflective glass.
From the first, you offer us ellipses,
long dashes, and *like time itself* the space
of triple spacing inside which a phrase
frays. The spacing grows longer. You whisper
death and birth in winged scripts and hospital
familiarities; no guarantee
of arriving *pulsed and present*; except
via soft, often unrelated forms:
phoneless phonetics, *limb-like* roots, typed words.

Halfway through *Us*, considering your name's
origins, your poem passes into
Urdu lovesong; quits that for *Yrs affec*,
the abbreviated signoff archived
in an English novelist's hand; which leads
to another correspondence, letters
to *letters – their afterlife –* , childlike
loss of consonants, how everything dis-
connects in the yellow airy treehouse
of your multifoliate verse, where to climb
a wardrobe is to find a family Quran

fittingly high from the ground, while to touch
wood is to happen on branchy Narnia.
Ishq: love: *ish*: halfway misunderstanding,
assent accented into ascent, *tall*
kahani, a word for 'story' I heard first
and now always in old-time filmi song.
Y, y, y, in the *whirl* of your *world*
are briefer forms seeded with unfoldings:
us the well of *undulations*, the ink
of *unsure*, the dip of the *universe*.
Pronoun transmuted by vowel to verb,
Ys, ice of the *year* on Oðinn's ash-tree
Yggdrasill, highlighter 'y', adverbial
ending eeling *wordlessly, possibly*
away; and the arms that open are *yours,*
ours, a father layer, Zaf's sky map.

from **THE END OF THE POEM**

I

The end of the poem
The end of the poem happened before
The end of the poem happened before it
The end of the poem happened before it began
The end of the poem accumulates
The end of the poem culminates
The end of the poem fulminates
The end of the poem accumulates tales.
It queues. It comes late. It tails
off. And on. And anon.

II

The end of the poem happened before it began,
when I was not but in the eye of an audience
I. It is done. The poem is Trinidadian,
is double x chromosomed, is one hundred and fifty cm,
is creatively crushing on a dead Scottish man
and imagines itself in medieval Italian
and is none of I, Lord have mercy, it is not what I am.

III

The end of the poem happened
when it had a procedure,
when it was put together
without having been taken apart

with only a being apart and partial
ever conceived for conceded to celebrated by what
it was not nor was nor was within nor was within it.
For example, the poem is prophesied at random,
by the painless unpicking of lexicons.
Take the seventh word down from
    l'articulation
          the seventh word down from
               manager ou manageur
             word
                  exorbitant, exorbitante
                down from
                  pondérateur,
                    pondératrice
I said, take the seventh word down from
    reclusion
        hot damn!
           tortillon
Who said which language
the book had to be in, anyway?

IV

Fuck that shit. Now that's a poem.
Fuck that capitalist imperialist military-industrial-complex
sexist skinniest lyricist white supremacist escapologist
pissed invisibilist againstist swerfy terfy resentful
ampersand prizewinning mainstream linear development
poor projection low sillage imitation civet hydrogenated
nooclear shit. – That sentence has a direct object.
Fuck syntax. – Imperative. Direct object.
Examine – okay, examining, build up the – no, definite article,
direct object – you know what I'm getting at ?!
you?! I?! Pro. Pronominal. Pro. Prostitutional.

Prostitinstitutional. Pronominanimal. Proem.
It's getting there. CUT! This is a poem. CUT! Ape 'em.

v

Every poem an ouroboros.
The beginning of the poem,
its tightest overlap, expansile rainbow,
scaly pacifier, nubbed
into its jaw,
teeth sheathe the teat
that is tail in mouth
and amoral slippage,
infinite tonguetwister,
untranslatable in transit
between high-spec
contingent integument,
the noun it is born to,
and the time it's unthought for.

POEMIME

after Theatre Re and Étienne Decroux

Your head is a question mark.
Your neck cannot rotate.
Your heart is the laziest part of your body.
Your arms are dust.
Your waist cannot rotate.
There is a champagne bottle between your legs.
Good quality champagne,
not cheap prosecco.
Your head snaps back.
When you tried to be
a little bit unbalanced,
that was nice.

MIDNIGHT ROBBER MONOLOGUE

The Midnight Robber takes to the streets in Trinidad and Tobago. Skulls and ruined structures hang from his sombrero. The winnings of his robberies underpin the gorgeous satin and fringes of his black cloak, wide as a condor's wings, lined with a colour and decorations like the sunset over lying and murderous nations. He lifts his knees high, higher in his tall boots. He carries a weapon, a gun or a cutlass, ready to chop-up or to shoot. His whistle shatters the air. Robbers duel in Tamarind Square, challenging each other with their sweeping actions and speeches that beat back the aeroplane Concorde breaking the sound barrier, leaving it stuck behind like a pram abandoned by its carrier. Robbers hold up the crowd of revellers. Is this Death the Cowboy? No. The Robber is older than you can ever understand. He seizes the present. He is Fear itself. He is the eternal shadow underpinning all the five continents' shifty land.

HALT! Make way for the STRANGER INVADER. I am the darkness that invades your mind. You are the darkness that is mine.

In the time when allyuh gods was a mist kissing the arse of the black water that covered the face of the world with all the green dolor, I was the astronomical anti-matter. Where the angels glide and collide with me I smash up the angels to eternity.

Before the earth rise up as god's son and daughter, I dry up god's tears and eat up their laughter. I was the hurt that hobble the angel foot. I was the rot that spread in the forest's root.

Who ever try to count and plan out night and day, minute and hour, I was before: nanosecond and nanofirst and Nani wine and Nanny of the Maroons are infants to me, for I am the error that recurs to infinity.

I am the nerves that push the mad president's hand to push the button. I am the last words that you forget to utter, I when you negotiating the last chance to save your sister or your mother. I am the hostility in the hostage situation, and the hostage situation is where I lead every nation.

I have no genealogy, I am the play with no rules and real corpses, the universal unbalance of gains and losses.

Tremble before me, the STRANGER INVADER.

I take every shape and no shape. I am obstacle everlasting that tricks those who want to be free. I destroy time, I am the horror you cannot keep away, I am the sentence with words of snakes that bind and rape up the judge on judgement day, I am the gramoxone love song at the wedding of the doctor, I am the child bride hymen beneath the fingernails of the lawyer, I am the coat hanger in the cupboard of the priest wife room, I am the terrorist vampire from the Lapeyrouse tomb.

I erase your face where you seeing race.

There is nowhere to hide because I am inside you at a cellular level, splitting your atoms in a nuclear evil.

I am the mangrove's inside-out womb, I bring the foreign submarine to honeymoon under your waterline, I give your sons a submachine and make them feel how it have plenty bullets, so they use it like a love machine.

It is futile to hide, I am death multiplied.

I am as small as the smallpox in a blanket. You feel you are big but you are only big like bullshit.

You have nowhere to hide. The STRANGER INVADER owns your field.

My steel boot tramples down your football pitch till it becomes a parade ground for every bitch who sees race. I come, I seize and I erase.

I am curare on an arrow that a parent brings to school, I am plastic spikes in ocean fish you swallow like a fool. I am the chlorine quiet quiet in the family murder swimming pool. I drown you in a quarter syringe of sea. Do not forget that you belong to me.

When Columbus men landed holding their bright weapons up, I was waiting for them in the form of dew and rust. When the British and the Spanish and the French and the Dutch and the Yankees and the Portuguese took away your language, I grew strong eating your tongues. I am the fatigue that waits in the cheap aeroplane and causes it to crash. I am the biological vector that turns the suicidal farmer's harvest to ash. I am the force that shatters the astronomer of freedom's telescope to splinter in his eye, I am the widespread lack of education that blind your comrade and make him cry, I am the expert in outing off your people's hope. I am the top freemason Cardinal of Robbers. I elect and poison and beget every Robber pope.

At the age of minus six hundred and sixty six, I met the seraphim and cut off their pricks. At the age of minus seven, I cast down heaven into the Labasse. At the age of zero I forged my own cutlass. At the age of five I took your life, and your life, and your life. Your lives were sweet, and zombification was complete. At the age of nine, darkness was all mine. From the age of ten I operate as a ageless robber douen.

There is nothing you can give me to make me forgive. Not your gold and not your soul. I already have them stacked up in my offshore currency.

III
SPARKS

SPARKS

Three playlets after Muriel Spark, in the form of surreal centos with original interludes, for several readers or performers and at least one singer.

AMUSEMENT, TO BEGIN: GOING DANCING

'The red shoe – '
'The brick.'
'The red shoe is – '
'The boat.' 🐸
'The red shoe has – '
'The boat has a frog – '
'The red shoe measures – '
'The boat has a green frog – '
'The shoe.'
'The red boat has a green frog on the side.'
'The slip-on.'
'The cherry tomato has white mildew across the top.'
'The size 38 El Naturalista – '
'The tent of oud and castoreum – '
'es "Una forma de ser. Una forma de pensar."'
'This will not make – '
'Advertising copy – '
'– a good description.'
'– indicates otherwise.'
'Otherwise,'
'The red shoe– '
Da capo al segno 🐸

I

It is important to recognise the years of one's prime by the fire that quickens Nilus' slime. But Safety does not come first – a vagabond flag upon the stream. Goodness, Truth and Beauty come first. Yea, like the stag, follow me when snow the pasture sheets; listen to me, with most delicious poison I would make of you the crème de la crème.

Green in judgment, she heard no screams. Cold in blood, she gave no scream; burnt on the water.

Infinite variety wore tweed or, at the most, musquash. Lustre that would do them all their days thickens. A double life of her own shines.

Dancing the tube in the flame, the gold I give thee will I melt and dozens of dancing green tubes and flames pour down thy ill-uttering throat.

Your hostages did the splits and the wild disguise made her laugh.

II

My cold heart? Famous. Let heaven, famous for gaudy night, call to me.

False, false won, her reputation. Like a man of steel, Sandy wanted sport. Sandy thought: *O infinite virtue, com'st thou sailing?* Looked back i' th' fire – understood, i' th' air – even more frightened, spoke; said, *water is in water...* started to hate black vesper's pageants.

Mussolini stood on a platform like him that loves me, a Gym teacher lock'd in her monument, or a Guides mistress darkling. The Castle, which was in any case everywhere the crown o' th' earth, rearing, doth melt.

III

'I'll be your man' – to rush into the secret house built so warningly
with equalness. Upraised fingers do that thing that ends.
I lead all their deeds. I thrust, stark-nak'd. Pray for the
Unemploy'd – is't not your trick?

All of a piece like one dragon's body which shall show the
cinders of my spirits, in the city Squeaking Cleopatra yet would not
go away: the worm's an old worm, and was unslayable.

Immortal longings in crowded fire and air – war-bereaved
spinsterhood a lover's pinch – the democratic counters of Edinburgh
grocer shops knot intrinsicate. Edinburgh a European capital...

Poor fig leaves, this prime of Miss Brodie's slime upon them.

IV

Trampled still in the making, our atavistic ennui launched the
Centaur's birth at the gates of life. Damn! Ouch!

Sing the love of danger as if Caesar sat there absolute; glorify
war, and scorn for woman.

I met a young poet by a fountain. Free this land from the
sinister promiscuity of painters and sculptors gradually turning
against ferocious slaughtering. Sex-bestirred object, in violent spasms
of action and creation, come on!

It was true. Set fire in verification, pitilessly eliminating the
doubts. Younger and stronger men don't believe. Trembling, believe.
Our images had magnetic properties when rubbed.

Injustice, good morning.

Strong and sane, in order to restore decency you meditate
upon the swan.

Hurl our defiance, united and alert, to the stars.

V

In the process of moving the cake, the most powerful cyclone originated. Disturbance identified a horrible creature. Tracking a terrible beast, by this time she looked quite beautiful and frail. Forecasters, without implicating themselves, killed 600 people just to see if it could be done by sheer looking. Maintaining its peak intensity, the Brodie set influenced the system. Hurricane structure was a real renunciation.

Extensive losses in her prime gradually followed, a strong tropical depression at other times letting the bell scream on. The system passed over uncertainty: 'Hitler *was* rather naughty'. This conflicts with a pressure to retire, made aware that sustained power lines wreaked havoc.

The control tower had been teaching fascism.

In a local cemetery, fallen trees were dispatched on many occasions and failed their tireless work of heavy deposits. Elsewhere, a plane crash marked the centre's archive.

'There was a Miss Jean Brodie in her prime.'

SOURCES: Muriel Spark, *The Prime of Miss Jean Brodie*. William Shakespeare, *Antony and Cleopatra*. F.T. Marinetti translated by R.W. Flint, *The Futurist Manifesto*. Wikipedia page for Hurricane Debbie (1961), accessed 17.00 on 7 August 2018: https://en.wikipedia.org/wiki/Hurricane_Debbie_(1961)

See you when I get back.
I have fallen in love with your silence.
Why are your arms so thin?
You are better looking than I am.
Are you a student?
I didn't used to like barbaric jewellery,
but since meeting you
I've changed my mind.
There's a piece of land I want to buy,
but I don't have capital; do you
have capital?
You need to get rid of some of these books.
Happy Valentine's Day.
I want a cigarette.
Do you know her?
You remind me of her.
I used to visit her
in her flat
and we'd meditate.
You're roaring.
Does it hurt you to roar?
Why are you stretching your leg
as if you want to kick somebody?
You are a gentle person.
You are a teacher.
You dress
like the daughter of a teacher.
Didn't your mother teach you
to cook ethnic food?
Why no books in the bathroom?
Are you genuinely happy with him?

I like canoeing, beekeeping,
and writing evil-woman songs,
and I travel with my own fold-up bike.
You'd need to become a Catholic,
but you wouldn't mind that.
Of course we shall be companions until death.
I am the poet of your spirit.
Don't forget me. Don't ever
forget me.
Don't ever forget.
I enjoyed our long walks.
Why do people talk so much about Hitler?
Why don't you hear them talking about Stalin?
My family were aristocrats.
We had much bigger windows than yours.
We are very different people.
Do you really believe that?
I don't think she meant it that way.
You don't really believe that.
Why are those girls dressed like hookers?
I am sitting here looking at you
without the slightest desire to kiss you.
Why do they want to get married?
Wow, that dress makes you look hefty!
I have activities on Sunday;
I can't schedule in the seaside.

I

The other servants fell silent, as circulation and disruption is not the only threat. Like plum-trees that grow crooked over standing pools: poison'd, beauteous, melancholy.

Shutting her eyes, she says: 'If there shall arise you, a prophet, or a dreamer of dreames, and if you must have coloured rope, you have been long in France.'

He speaks with other tongues. 'Only technically is the not impossible, possible. You incline to shed blood – cherries in cognac, terrible carrots, and there's the blender in front of you. I was lured to you, according to the body alone, your blindfolded partner.'

The other servants fall silent in a general eclipse. Like moths in cloth, silkysmooth flame-meltable fibre.

He says: 'All week in my dreams I've heard spirits and diuels, the early darkening of violence. I can manage going mad. If we're lucky, there's still the engend'ring of toads, nylon, cotton and hemp, a bundle of bank-notes, with a dead policeman like a politic dormouse. English is the higher-income language. Stop your mouth. Discern by a kind of X-ray eye.'

She says, 'Out of brave horsemanship arise the first sparks of sex, according to the body and soul together. The stomach moves in riddles and in dreams, of such mixed nationalities, between the past, present and future tenses.'

Impossible actions, some of metal, some of leather, behind the arras. It's day and night with lycanthropia. Sex is not to be read i' th' stars. Raise it higher. Sex is nothing but a howl and a clatter, a terrible dream, never enough ice. Keep close. First lightly melt into the possessed mans body, under any twisting force. Are we happy here? Multiply the points of tension before we die. Pain's nothing.

He leaves. He didn't live to eat a mere stick of sugar-candy, the idiot boy's supper.

Him in the attic is not in nature. Him in the attic was sure to be something unexpected. Him in the attic, the human form, verie certeine I am, is frozen into marble.

'Somewhat radiant quick-sands essentially transforme themselues into precautions,' says his aunt Eleanor.

II

It is ten-thirty at night. Lister has changed. 'I can shape myself to make it symmetrical, vtterly impossible, transmuted, transfashioned, transfigured, transformed, or metamorphozed.'

'When in hell did I say we are forc'd to express a miracle of Kindred and Affinity?'

As if for guidance they walk hand in hand with nonslip properties, create a tight loop, its dangling filigree of wylie practizes. One shrill owl-screech: 'What an unskilful fellow!' Another shrill breath smells of lemon-pills. The bell shrills, attached by a long snaky cord to a scribbling block here in the gallery dangling, dangling, dangling, banging, ringing, lapping, lulling, sleeping, scrambling, waiting.

'Sticke fast. It hasn't happened.'

'And you have a hotel to be made sweet, the sunken rose garden, your shrimp-pink marriage-bed, pink blond apricocks, white mink bubbles of water.'

'It's going to happen.'

Voices rebound: 'They are a free state, sir. There have been telephone conversations throughout.' 'Poor thing in the attic.' 'A sad case.' 'Bind this. Repeat the operation on a miniature scale, gracefully, freshly, conceivably, cleverly, swiftly, luminously green.' 'Sheepskin.' 'Wolfskin.' French courtiers side-track the climax. Taste of musk. You use them and throw them away.

A bit hungry, the machine, hairy on the outside, emits a nose of wax. A nose of wax glitters obliquely.

'Your dreams give me different furniture.'

The shots being fired, what power lightens in great men's breath?

Not to disturb. Far into the night, the books are silent, resist unwinding themselves. Probably the library released many lines. Open the loops. It could take all night. Achieve this woven diamond, and still more chaos effectively to organise.

III

'It must have happened quick. Old friends, like old swords, cut away occasion. Successive twists simply spiralled together.'

'Who desired occasion?'

'The physicians transformed into wolves. It is quite relevant to the practices that go on without my knowledge.'

'Intelligence will freeze his long spell of dancing.'

Fear, quite a thrilling emotion, made him invisible, monstrous, vulturous.

'Lights there, lights!'

'Is the Baron breathing for certaine?'

'Does a flame feel pain?'

'Love mix'd with fear. The same golden showers.'

'The camera puts me in mind of death.'

'Put your finger through the eye of all the officers o' th' court.'

'Fish your fingers through the V made by her belly which moves, absurdly and grossely.'

As he rocks, the sound of the motor recedes. Throttle it, winding frailty folded in nobility, winding absolutely, really, languidly, fondly, silently.

The devil is cunning enough, carrying on in the library. I seek no windings or turnings at all, when you relate a small press-cutting. I don't relate the stark-naked tape recorder. How was't possible she got hook'd on the shininge of a glass, strangling my shadow? Vile woman!

'The Reverend should catch our purpose.'

They went to prison for, yes, sex. A first-rate movie script that's already flown. Adjust the new anti-sex masks and curtains, which flatly auoucheth vnto vs: I want his head.

'Did you find the bunch of violets in the library?'

'Conclude what you please: yet plant my soul in mine ears.'

Meet on one centre. It is all tied up.

IV

At a quarter past seven, while the sky whitens, pearls give expressions of delight rather than pain to a dead man's skull. The rising of the wind bends an ear to Moscow, pianissimo, and an injection for controlling your adventure.

'What do you think of these, after the torso piece is clothed with the embroidered table cloth?'

'Oh, my dreams of the breaking open of the library door by diuels?'

Numerous precious vases crash to the floor. The journalists change into rhubarb, O, the pen in the giggler's hand digg'd up a mandrake. Feed the ropes down through the occasional howl. Feed the ropes up behind a Spanish fig and a howl. Feed the ropes down through flattery and lechery, and a howl.

'Don't let them out again. Impudent snake! I understand you want to remove any slack?'

'I mean not to publish ouer rashlie. Strict orders: open a space between the people's curses, securing urinals filled with rosewater.'

'The busy workers, fierce with trying, find it radical? Shameful ways. Lose no time. Adjust the tension.'

'I'd rather keep the police out of it. Keeping the tension, kill him.'

'His tape-recorder stol'n too. His camera, to priviledge errour.'

'It seemed a private whispering-room. Victor and the Baron can do a deal with a salamander's skin; let the bonds be forfeit.'

A tiny padlock. A very free agent. Touch the padlock. Transforme.

It can't be simplified without confusion of substances. Now take comfort, weeping but not helping. A dead thing unforeseen, Greensleeves. Lust. A dead thing unforeseen, Greensleeves. Combust. Pornophilia does not make for a bird more beautiful, enamoured to the brim with voluntary torture.

'I am perplexed,' says the Reverend.

A night-walker, glittering with ecstatic gladness, cut with our own dust, is not to be disturbed. Come on, Lycanthropus. Shall I never fly in pieces? Tell him I want to see him when he wakes up.

V

'Bear in mind,' says Lister, 'that when dealing with the rich, apply desperate physic; a sexy application, in gold and sugar.'

'Clara has had dreams, excellent hyena, terrible dreams, in such a deformed silence.'

'Our position of privilege is purchas'd honour, large green grapes, any grapes. The door is locked, to ensure circulation.'

'Wondrous strange. Death hath ten thousand several doors, and a tiny pair of scissors (depending on the length of your rope).'

'The keys are banish'd.'

'Strangers aren't permitted: balsamum, a litter of porcupines, folly, tyranny, frailty, curiosity, melancholy, safety, calamity. A dismal kind of music, the master key. Keep them happy, modestly, tremulously, quaveringly waiting for the relief man to come.'

'A not-so-simple conundrum. For the wild consort of reporters with their microphones and cameras, full of daggers, have cast the same into a serpentine colour.'

'A shameful act of sin! Bury the print of it in a terrible place, terrible places. My Monet and my Goya are Duchess of Malfi still.'

'Send them away.'

An inspector of police, a thing of sorrow, a police detective, a general mist of error, two plain-clothes men, too much i' th' light, three uniformed policemen, true substantial bodies and a police photographer bound to enjoy strangling, by an vnorderly course of zig-zags, troop in.

'No shots? Journalists are killed without pain.'

'I will first receive my pension.'

'Mercy! The bodies are confiscated, stowed away in soft lint, in a large dark red stain.'

'She takes them for that body of hers, wild-fire well splashed with his blood.'

The camera flicks imperceptibly. Refusing comment. Like a bloody fool...

'Now you know directly they are Daemonium Lupinum. A wooluish Demoniacke. Ravens, sharper than sunbeams. Lupina melancholica. A rope-maker. Lupina insania. A wooluish melancholie. Sparks of roughness, with sleeplessness in their movements and on their faces. A wooluish furie and madness. Cover her face. Mine eyes dazzle into a verie natural woolfe.'

'If they would bind me to a wild night, I have so much obedience in my blood.'

'And what meane you by the power of obedience?'

Looking towards the library, I myself am essentially transformed into a woolfe.

Outside the house the sunlight is laughing on the walls.

SOURCES: Muriel Spark, *Not to Disturb*. John Deacon and John Walker, *Dialogicall Discourses of Spirits and Divels*. John Webster, *The Duchess of Malfi*. Two Knotty Boys and Larry Utley, *Two Knotty Boys Showing You the Ropes*.

INTERLUDE: SHIBARINA FAIR, ENTWISTED BRIDE OF LULLINGS: A SEXTINA

what x c z is what y get,
& she is at her rope's end.
descripointment sol far, vert visible,
her her invested in invisible,
everray seemeth green in spathes ae tree:
seven metres hempen two stockinette feet.

verboten dizzy thocht, her digital feet –
moss inside must surface, amosset, get
tinniculation, millial blood-tree
paracordialement branchit, sew end
loops loupsen furnthest, nerfs' invisible
conference spiels ideographs, visible

fanspokes shet up syllables en visible
felinity, subdued; her shy braid feet
perfect-bound, subeditive, invisible
as 'like', a monoslickable. get
thes smileyly: rinse & wring & end
inwraptruest editude: a cordage tree.

forget the girl, the ropes, also the tree
qhere lafes fele haver, grnees skeen visible,
chafeinches snikk taether fringers' end,
altellidicates fervified feet –
sequoia una fantasia, yew get
equiangels of the invisible,

tensile exchange betwine invisible
end eravasable sashyneinge tree

exclusive of amussed faerielint. get
a grip, the pore fing's pallor's visible,
impalisadoed & entreed. her feet
wore excellent until the end:

rammementizati: sic an end!
rapidoing two unstarry rigs, did invisible
madamage tae her peerless feet.
sheerly alone, a sailor sings a tree
hugge lullables, his landlove visible,
tho he's seldom mewse enough tae get

heavy lines get down split
light end visible; eða rock
silly pets nibbling invisible tree feet.

'You dirty swine. Stand, and unfold yourself.'

'To be quite frank, I won't. That were both stiff and stowre.'

'Let us once again assail your ears that are so fortified against our story. You may be asked at an interview what thing it is that a woman will most desire.'

King Arthur then hit him. The baron hit back. The affair is a legend.

The cock crew had known all Peckham.

'Thy ransome, cone-winder, trainee-seamer, process-controller, up-twister, packer, gummer.'

'You're a dirty swine. You, your experience and your knowledge of the pubs.'

'Say what? Show your expertise.'

'It wouldn't have happened, poor ghost, if you could choose something lawless you are particularly proud of.'

And Elsie, whose sore task does not divide the Sunday from the week, said, 'No, I'm sweating.'

'Tush. Hold my piece. Under two minutes.'

The interviewer is not looking for the gang at the Elephant. Those shoes were old. The air bites. Unfledg'd comrade so bright of blee, don't rush the fruitful river in the eye, the act of fear.

'You have researched the organisation, wide and full of white young teeth.'

'O peace, O peace. Always be prepared to research into the real Peckham.'

'No, quite honestly, thou comest in such a questionable shape, I won't.'

'Just out of National Service, Sir Gawaine?'

In feeding the line wings, praise be to the Lord. In feeding the line skills, you must show that you are proactive. In feeding the line jelly, I feel I'm your man. Nothing swete.

'Tomorrow I wold fight.'

'Tomorrow I shold begone.'

Working culture is boiling, expansion plans boiling over. It needed the bit of fretful porpentine, sweating, standing stiffe and strong.

She cried: 'The meadows are open, of thy owne hearts desiring, lion's nerve. I must come againe; having some mermaiden scruples, swim into the hands of concealed lighting.' She was cladd in maggots.

'Your proudest achievement...?'

'Nothing to be a snob about. '

'Moult no feather! Tell a story. Begin by explaining her mouth, her eye, curteouslye.'

'Getting too sexy.'

'Similar to the challenges you might face if like a crab you could go backward. Think of a recent problem to be a snob about.'

No snob, mincing with his sword, poses like an angel-devil. There are classes within classes in Peckham. Nipping, smiling, not smiling, performing the twisting jive, merging the motions of the fight, living a lie, give statistics and figures, lose the support of your unions. Focus on arbitration in trade disputes. End with hard words. An Okapi is a rare beast to ease thee of thy paine.

The action you took hasn't any railings.

'Vision,' said Mr Druce, with a great weapon. 'Lawful espials.'

'Vision,' Dougal said, standing stiff and stronge. 'I must be idle. You are a good listener. Yeeld thee, in a natural way.'

'I am tame, sir: you led a team. Pronounce. Nickname God's creatures.'

'Suggestions: Come and leap, leopard. Questions: Feeling frail, nightingale? Got a pain, panda? An interviewer will be able to tell.'

Hoold his hand. For this is not thy ransome sure. Cheer in prison a good browne sword. Hover over me with your wings, Boudicca. Believe in the Devil? Quack, quack. Quack, quack. Quack, quack. The end of your interview. Believe in the Devil, by Vision?

Frost itself as actively doth burn.
To speake my mind – my words fly up –
Peckham must have a king.

'You are going to face thieves of mercy, out at tea break;
industrial discontents in red scarlett; politic worms...'
Mortal and unsure, the brave beast emphasises the word
'immoral'. Praise be to the Lord psychologically, socially. You like
to know the word 'ignorant'.
'Absenteeism. A thirteen-year-old blackmailer. There's a
place in Soho, a misshapen, evil place in Soho.'
'I get that excited by Holy Scripture, an early vengeance.'
'A chance for promotion in the future, incorpsed and
demi-natured.'
'I see a lady, a diabolical agent.'
Profound heaves.
'A woman will haue her will.'
'In a fyer I will her burne.'
Convocation of clean dirt. Yes. Yes, yes.

A bright spiky chandelier and sheepksins. Grey teamwork,
red company, grey delivering, gold results, red commitment, white
reliability, red and white ventures, red-shaded calfskins. Groove
in. Groove in. You look awful. This grave shall have a living
monument. Illness is abhorrent. Vnseemly. A fatal flaw.
'How doth the job fit into the bodies of two lorries?'
'People can find out all about you. Code word, forrest.'
'Code word, chough.'
'Autumn's a clue. An act hath three branches.'
Maimed rites. She squirmed. Screamed. There was a kind
of fighting. 'Take your hands off me,' she said. 'Was heaven
ordinant...'
'Very sorry, good.'
Afraid – Who's afraid, whosoeuer kisses – Not afraid of his
kiss – Afraid of his kiss - Whosoeuer kisses the breathing-time of

day, we defy augury. We'll go into the boat.

Question is, what game of sex, fox? Question is, national or international, bugs and goblins? What's a doughnut to a kid? Fresh.

Some tooke vp their hawks, money-mad. Some tooke vp their hounds, money in their pockets. How would you describe the poor devil? Soft! Not at work. Soft! Too upset to work. Peckham. A positive environment. There are simply no people in the place; a paid police informer choose thee! A private word in the diuells name. She screamed with hysterical mirth, eager to hear their analysis.

'A good self-manager has some tiny reservations about the Peckham bits.' She started crying.

The great throbbing heart of London across the river spelt pearl, palpable truth.

One soe milde of moode stabbed silence into her long neck. Private business, when lords chucked, kicked, grabbed, held att this time an appreciation; clutching all the coins and the old bronze stumbled, grabbed and juggled with some carefully chosen shin bones, fled from hencforth out of Peckham with something to remember us by.

'I can't stop to assist you.'

Barbary horses taking Denmark Hill.

'I must hyde my selfe.'

There was Dixie come up to the altar with an old knight. Pass with your best violence off to Africa with the intention of selling your strengths.

'Chance fortune? My interest in a young lady…'

'No, better systems, to be quite frank.'

Woe, a dirty swine must walke the green forrest; a feend of hell finish on a high.

'In fact they witched me, witched new ideas for robbing a till. The drum rejoyced all that day.'

You are the right person for another world than this. Glad as grass wold be of raine, go swiftly past the Rye, looking like silence.

SOURCES: Muriel Spark, *The Ballad of Peckham Rye. The English and Scottish Popular Ballads*. Ed. Francis James Child. 5 vols. Boston, MA, and New York: Houghton, Mifflin, and Co., 1883–1898. William Shakespeare, *Hamlet*. http://www.direct.gov.uk/articles/common-interview-questions (Accessed 13 November 2018.)

Transform one word into another, one letter at a time.
See if you can make a word into its opposite!

JEST
JUST
DUST

MOLE
MOLT
MOAT
GOAT

SWORD
SWORE
SHORE
CHORE
CHOSE
CHASE
PHASE
PEASE
PEACE

SWEAR
SWEAT
SWEET
SHEET
SLEET
FLEET
FLEES
FREES
TREES
TRESS

DRESS
DROSS
GROSS
GRASS
GLASS
GLANS
GLAND
GRAND
GRANT
GRUNT
BRUNT
BLUNT
BLENT
BLEAT
BLEST
BLESS

IV
ASTRONOMER OF FREEDOM

SYNTAX POEMS: MAKING MULTIVOCAL PERFORMANCE TEXTS

The writer Martin Carter (1927–1997) was involved in the conscious creation of Guyana, from revolutionary times and his jail writings to his representative later roles, from government minister to beloved regional poet. He was sensitive to the histories inscribed in his, and any, land as 'tongueless whispering'. Today's Caribbean is no less animated and inscribed by the 'shape and motion' of Carter's language. His original audiences could recite his poems by heart. Nowadays his words continue to make their way into genuinely popular song, protest and performance, for example during the curfew-challenging event in Trinidad in 2011, 'I Dream to Change the World'.

Why then my transreading of Carter to produce new 'syntax poems' for performance, when his work is still alive, still carrying out its own propulsive transformation?

From 2014 to 2016, during and after my Judith E. Wilson Poetry Fellowship at the University of Cambridge, I had access to a blackbox studio theatre, a dark space with insulated walls and movable seating. With a group of people including genius theatre maker Jeremy Hardingham and brilliantly inventive students Paige Smeaton and Hope Doherty, I started to evolve a way of immersing audiences in the feeling of the world of a poem, rather than staging standard readings of texts (microphone and lectern, audience forced to face one way and be worshipful). We were not interested, either, in a conventional dramatisation of a poetic script. Instead, immersive experiments became the context for events including reading of full texts alongside what I call 'syntax poems' gleaned from them. The syntax poems offer traces of a way of being *with and inside* Carter's poetry. They are not the kind of independent verbal artefacts called responses or reworkings. They are rearrangeable elements for future experiments. They require several voices. They are best realised via bodies in motion.

One of our primary desires in creating these syntax poems was to free a feeling of movement to rise out of Carter's words. Carter's poetry is restless and has been recited in conditions of unrest. Being alone with a book prioritises its equally valuable, but less excitable, aspects. A solo reader might pause over the density of Carter's language. Its fishermen, protesters, flowers and streets are evocative, symbolic, yet specific. Place ingrained in feeling seems to encourage researched reading. Sparse details can be unfurled into Guyanese realities. We, on the contrary, appreciated without wanting to dwell.

How to attain the desired feeling of movement? In transreading Carter to produce syntax poems, we concentrated on features of the language where activity happens, such as verbs and prepositions. For example, the Creole verb form 'I come' can mean 'I came' or 'I come'; in a poem, an understanding of this doubleness may allow past and present to co-exist. Another example: Carter's incantatory, obsessive joining or piling up of elements by 'in' or 'of' can feel overwhelming, like a kind of tilting of the poetic ground. We wanted to induce that vertigo in the audience; we would not skip, like the eye can, over the *act* of joining in order to fetishise *what* is joined. Further, we also felt that Carter's 'I' is so often extensive, inclusive, that to embody his texts simultaneously in various overlapping readings and actions might produce more of a sense of the *I that can be we* than any amount of explanation could.

Together and alone, silently and aloud, we kept re-reading selected Carter texts, at first 'simply' for syntax and features which activate movement. We did not care to 'shred', 'collage' or 'fracture'. Fearfully and lovingly, with the energy of our watered, out-of-breath bodies and voices, we tried to uncover, create and assemble mobile skeletons and provocative patterns of words, with enough colourful shreds of 'meaning' for the audience to follow the dance.

Carter's long poem, 'I Am No Soldier', which ends with the famous summoning of an 'astronomer of freedom' and secular hymn to the glittering potentiality seeded in ourselves, passes from a recognisably Guyanese opposition of soldiers in a jungle to poets in jail cells, through now challenging sections (praise of Mao Tse Tung...) and vast visions of resistance that call on named parts of the world, to the politically engaged *and* aesthetically-driven artist's conclusion 'I am this poem like a sacrifice'. We decided to invite whatever Cambridge audience we could muster into the world of this work. We also decided to be true to our own backgrounds, bringing in individual ways of connecting with or departing from the text, in the belief that a vivid self-honesty might electrify the audience into their own revulsions or connexions.

It was important to re-present Carter's world/work in ways that would be recognisable to readers who have grown up with his words and are linked to his region, yet which those entirely unfamiliar with it would be free to enter.

As people filed into the blackbox, finding scant seating facing no particular way, they were distracted from the fact that a long fence of sharp wire hived off much of the right length of the room. To their left was a schoolroom, where tall Jeremy in the form of a colonial schoolmaster used his beautiful voice to berate and question two students, teaching them prescriptively about Martin Carter's poems and the right way to interpret them. This was as close as the audience got to a 'straight' reading. The lesson was not entirely oppressive nonsense; we made sure to smuggle in useful background information about Carter, his poetics and his time. This was justifiable, also being part of the play.

Like any good colonial schoolmaster, Jeremy failed to notice that the students, Hope and Paige, were dressed as mimes. Their answers turned increasingly unruly and imaginative – true to another aspect of Carter, his naturally enigmatic and quasi-modernist intellectual approach to innovation, in direct line from fellow Guyanese poet A.J. Seymour, with whom T.S. Eliot had corresponded. Eventually the mimes broke down the classroom and escaped.

During this time, dressed in white, I wandered through the studio like an itinerant preacher from a Welsh tradition of which Paige had told me, and which sparked associations for me with rhapsodic and ecstatic spiritual traditions in the Caribbean. In the style of a

Carter-crazed divine, I recited 'I Am No Soldier' from memory, in its entirety and in fragments, over and over again, as if trying to convert, inspire or intimidate my fellows. This character allowed me to sound the poem in its full sonority and musicality.

Moving from the schoolroom to the street – spaces of Carter's society – we quick-changed in the open centre of the blackbox. Suddenly appearing as would-be revolutionaries and persecuted ordinary folk, we were in the jail and the yard, inside and outside the barbed wire, making poem-placards.

We passed through other movement, vocal and costume sequences. We hoped to make the text inhabit areas of life and styles of being human and verbal that make sense in the world of 'I Am No Soldier', but which would be invisibilised in a lectern reading to the seated bodies of listeners. We paid homage to the polytheisms of the Caribbean, having a ceremony in which we passed out and came to life again ridden by Carter, whispering and chanting antiphonal syntax poems, our stripped-down word-patterning, so that they were less versions than manifestations, and the airy structure of his meanings began to rise and swing. Finally, we danced the dance of constellations, holding on to each other's long black and silver scarves, calling on the astronomer of freedom, rejoicing beyond all bounds and including anyone in the audience who wished to take part.

The audience effectively heard the whole text delivered in several different modes, as well as gaining an insight into symbolic and representative social environments *by being in them with us* and *having them co-exist in one blackbox*. They also heard a living, not anatomised, version of practical criticism and close reading – which is what the syntax poems also offer.

Although the syntax poems themselves are divided up on the page less like projective poetry than perhaps like medieval polyphony, ideally realised by at least two voices, it is crucial to remember that they do emerge from a linear reading of the source texts. When printed out, they look misleadingly like a sequence. Their intended effect arrives if words jump and jumble on the page in a way that informs the performance, and if the audience does not feel they have listened to 'readers of poetry', but rather participated in a sense of call and response, cry and chorus, intimate camaraderie. We hope this may be an invitation to others not only to read Carter, but to bring the life in poetry (not 'bring poetry to life'!) into immersive and visionary spaces.

The full text of 'I Am No Soldier' is reproduced here, followed by the syntax poems. After these is a sample of the rough notes by which we generated the syntax poems through close readings, and created scenes for the performance from memories of real-life places and situations.

I AM NO SOLDIER

Wherever you fall comrade I shall arise
Wherever and whenever the sun vanishes into an arctic night
there will I come.
I am no soldier with a cold gun on my shoulder
no hunter of men, no human dog of death.
I am my poem, I come to you in particular gladness
In this hopeful dawn of earth I rise with you dear friend.

O comrade unknown to me falling somewhere in blood.
In the insurgent geography of my life
the latitudes of anguish
pass through the poles of my frozen agonies, my regions of grief.
O my heart is a magnet
electrified by passion emitting sparks of love
Swinging in me around the burning compass of tomorrow
and pointing at my grandfather's continent, unhappy Africa
unhappy lake of sunlight
moon of terror...

But now the huge noise of night surrounds me for a moment
I clutch the iron bars of my nocturnal cell

peeping at daylight.
There is a dark island in a dark river
O forest of torture
O current of pain and channel of endurance
The nausea of a deep sorrow hardens in my bowels
And the sky's black paint cracks falling into fragments
Cold rain is mist! is air, is all my breath!

There is a nightmare bandaged on my brow
A long hempen pendulum marks the hour of courage
Swinging over the bloody dust of a comrade
one minute and one hour and one year
O life's mapmaker chart me now an ocean
Vast ship go sailing, keel and metal rudder.

It began when the sun was younger, when the moon was dull
But wherever you fall comrade I shall arise.
If it is in Malaya where new barbarians eat your flesh, like beasts
I shall arise.
If it is in Kenya, where your skin is dark with the stain of famine
I shall arise.
If it is in Korea of my tears where land is desolate
I shall wipe my eyes and see you
Comrade unknown to me...

I will come to the brave when they dream of the red and yellow
        flowers blooming in the tall mountains of their nobility...
I will come to each and to every comrade led by my heart
Led by thy magnet of freedom which draws me far and wide
over the sun's acres of children and of mornings...

O wherever you fall comrade I shall arise.
In the whirling cosmos of my soul there are galaxies of happiness
Stalin's people and the brothers of Mao Tse-tung
And Accabreh's breed, my mother's powerful loin

And my father's song and my people's deathless drum.
O come astronomer of freedom
Come comrade stargazer
Look at the sky I told you I had seen
The glittering seeds that germinate in darkness
And the planet in my hand's revolving wheel
and the planet in my breast and in my head
and in my dream and in my furious blood.
Let me rise up wherever he may fall
I am no soldier hunting in a jungle
I am this poem like a sacrifice.

Martin Carter

I AM NO SOLDIER: SYNTAX POEMS

I

Wherever   (Wherever you fall)
Wherever   (Wherever and whenever)
           there will I come

somewhere   (somewhere in blood)
           (in...In...through...Swinging in me)

      But now (the huge noise)...for a moment
There is...   (in a dark river)
O
O

           (in my bowels)
           (falling into fragments)

There is a nightmare

      (when the sun was younger, when the moon was dull)
But wherever   (wherever you fall)
If it is
If it is in   (in Malaya)
If it is
If it is in   (in Kenya)
If it is
If it is in   (in Korea)
           where...
           where new barbarians eat your flesh
           where...where...
           where new barbarians...
           where your skin is dark with the stain of famine

where...where...where...
where...barbarians
where...famine
where land is desolate

when they dream (dream of the red and yellow flowers)

O wherever   (wherever you fall)

there are galaxies of happiness
                    (in darkness)
                    (in my hand's revolving wheel)
                    (in my breast)
                    (in my breast and in my head)
                    (and in my head and in my dream)
                    (and in my dream and in my furious blood)

wherever   (wherever he may fall)

II

you fall   I shall arise
                  there will I come
                  I am no soldier
                  I am my poem, I come to you
                  (I come to you in particular gladness)
                  I rise with you
                  (I rise with you dear friend)

(O comrade)
(O my heart)

                  I clutch the iron bars
                  (I clutch the iron bars of my nocturnal cell)

(O life's mapmaker)
(Vast ship)

you fall   I shall arise
                            I shall arise
                            I shall wipe my eyes and see you

                            I will come
                            (I will come to the brave when they dream)
                            I will come
                            (I will come to each and to every comrade)

(O wherever)
you fall   I shall arise
(O come astronomer of freedom)
(Come comrade stargazer)
(Look)
(Look at the sky)   I told you I had seen
                            (seen / The glittering seeds that germinate
                            in darkness)
(Let me rise up)

                            I am no soldier
                            I am this poem

III

(Wherever)
into an arctic night
        there
             with a cold gun
in particular gladness
In this hopeful dawn

             with you

(somewhere)
in blood
In the insurgent geography
(in the latitudes of anguish)
             through the poles (agonies)
             (through regions (grief))
in me
             around the burning (the burning compass)
             at my grandfather's continent
             (at...Africa)

             at daylight
             There
in a dark river
in my bowels
into fragments

             There
             on my brow
             over the bloody dust (dust of a comrade)

(But wherever)
             If
in Malaya

                    Where
                    If
in Kenya,
                    where

                                        with the stain of famine (dark
                                        with the stain)
                    If
in Korea
                    where

                    to the brave
in the tall mountains
                    to each
                    to every comrade (to each and to every comrade)
                    by my heart (led)
                    by thy magnet (led)
                    far and wide
                    over the sun's acres

(O wherever)
In the whirling cosmos
                    there
                    at the sky (Look)
in darkness (the glittering seeds)
in my hand's revolving wheel (the planet)
in my breast (the planet)
in my head
in my dream
in my furious blood
(wherever)
in a jungle (no soldier)
(this)   (like a sacrifice)

No Soldier

comrade:

no soldier, no hunter, no human dog

dear friend:

O comrade, O comrade unknown:
unhappy Africa, unhappy lake of sunlight
...

O life's mapmaker:
Vast ship:

comrade:
Comrade unknown to me
...

comrade:
deathless drum
astronomer of freedom
comrade stargazer
no soldier
...

comrade   I shall arise
an arctic night   there will I come
I am no soldier   (I am) no... (I am) no...
I am my poem

O comrade   (who is) unknown
                       (who is) falling somewhere
O my heart   is a magnet
                       (is) electrified
                       (is) emitting sparks
                       (is) Swinging...and (is) pointing

There is a dark island
Cold rain is mist! is air, is all my breath!

There is a nightmare   nightmare (that is) bandaged

when the sun was younger, when the moon was dull
comrade   I shall arise
If it is   I shall arise
If it is   I shall arise
If it is   skin is dark with the stain   I shall arise
If it is   land is desolate
I shall wipe my eyes   (I shall) see you
Comrade   (who is) unknown

I will come   red and yellow flowers (which are) blooming
I will come   to each and every comrade

comrade   I shall arise
there are galaxies of happiness
there are... people... (there are)... brothers... (there is) Accabreh's

breed... (there is) my mother's powerful loin... (there is) my father's
song.... (there is) my people's deathless drum

And the planet   (which is) in my hand's revolving wheel
and the planet   (which is) in... and (is) in... and (is) in...
                          and (is) in... my furious blood
I am no soldier   (who is) hunting
I am this poem   (that is)...sacrifice ((I am)...sacrifice)

                              VI

Wherever...
O...
But...
There...
It...
I...
O...

Soldier /
        Wherever

arise / Wherever,
come. / I
shoulder / no hunter
death / I am
gladness / In this
dear friend /
                O comrade
blood / in the insurgent
life / the latitudes
anguish / pass
grief / O

a magnet / electrified
of love / Swinging in
tomorrow / and pointing
Africa / unhappy
sunlight / moon
terror.../
      But now
a moment / I clutch
nocturnal cell / peeping at
daylight. / There is
river / O
torture / O
endurance / The nausea
my bowels / and the sky's
fragments / Cold
breath! /
      There is
my brow / A long hempen pendulum
courage / Swinging over
a comrade / one
year / O
an ocean / Vast
rudder /
      It began
dull / But wherever
arise. / If it is
like beasts / I shall
arise. / If it is
famine / I shall
arise. / If it is
desolate / I shall
see you / Comrade
me... /
      I will
their nobility / I will

my heart / Led
wide / Over
mornings.../
      O
arise / In the whirling
happiness / Stalin's
Mao Tse-tung / And Accabreh's
loin / And my father's
drum. / O
freedom / Come
stargazer / Look
I had seen / the glittering
darkness / And the planet
wheel / and the planet
head / and in
blood. / Let
fall / I am
a jungle / I am
sacrifice. //

THE COLONIAL SCHOOLMASTER AND THE MIMES
Rules for Creating a Martin Carter Classroom from
Memories of Convent Schooling in the Caribbean

CLASSROOM: There is a blackboard to the right of a rostrum (raised platform) where the teacher has a special desk and chair. Ranged in rows in front of it are old wooden double desks. You cannot change desk once you have chosen a desk at the start of term. You must have taken out all books and materials needed for class at the start of class. You may not open your desk without permission. You may not look out the windows on the side of the room facing the street or go on to the balcony on that side of the building. You may not leave the premises during school hours without written permission. All subjects are taught here except on the rare occasions when the language lab, Audiovisual room, science lab, art rooms, Activity Room, or music room, is scheduled for use ahead of time by the teacher. Home Economics is always in the Home Economics room, taught by the local nun who says that cooking is not finished until you have washed up. A petite Irish nun may on occasion schedule Religion in the Prayer Room, where you are required to genuflect on entry, exit and every time you pass directly in front of the Blessed Sacrament, which has not been housed in the Chapel since the fire long ago in which some nuns perished. She tells you that the French are sinful, and French is a sinful language. However, there is a lot of singing in Religion. You may ask for permission to use the Activity Room, music room, theatre, or lumber room with an old piano, if you have a high-level exam, competition, show or project in progress. If you are not Catholic, you may spend Religion period in the library. You may use the library only during breaktime, lunchtime, or the library period. Library studies are taught by another Irish nun, who teaches you the Dewey Decimal system, shows you a film about the Pope, and asks you to list all the sports the Pope plays. Chemistry is taught by yet another Irish nun, who has one flesh hand, one prosthetic hand covered by a glove. She rubs her hands together under the fluorescent strip lights when the lights flicker. She says this will jump-start them into steadiness, and that this is magic. You are not allowed to enter the central atrium of the school via the blue-carpeted stairs, or to check yourself into the sick room without permission. There is what seems to be the remnant of a prie-dieu in the sick room.

TIMETABLE: There is Assembly at 07.45 for 07.50 on Monday, Wednesday and Friday, and singing practice for all at the same time on Tuesday. If you are in the fourth form, there are no chairs. You must stand at the back. If you feel that you are going to faint, inform a prefect and leave quietly. The register is taken. Classes are 40 minutes long, separated by a bell. Break is from 10.10–10.20. Lunch is from 11.50–12.30 with prayers afterwards. You are not really expected to need the loo apart from these times, and certainly not to eat or drink.

CONDUCT IN CLASS, FOR STUDENTS: You will address all teachers as 'Miss', 'Mrs', 'Mr' or 'Sir', or 'Sister'. E.g. 'Good morning, Sister Paul.' 'Excuse me, Miss, please may I open my desk?' During class you will put your hand up and wait to be called before speaking to the teacher. When speaking to the teacher, you must be standing, and you must thank the teacher and sit down when finished. You may not speak to your classmates unless you are instructed to work together. You must not sit with your legs in a Y shape under the desk. At the beginning of class, you will all be seated in place. The teacher will enter. You will stand and greet her (or him): 'Good morning, Miss/Mrs/Sr/Mr (plus name)'. You will be required to repeat this if you do not speak clearly. You will sit when instructed to do so. The teacher or prefect will take the register. When your name is called, by surname, you will put your hand up and clearly say 'Present'.

CONDUCT IN CLASS, FOR THE TEACHER: It is possible to call students by Creole or other insults instead of their name, in an aggressive yet humorous voice, e.g. 'Coonoomoonoo!' 'Mook!' or simply 'Idiot'. You are not supposed to punish them physically but may give them extra homework or lines to write, send them to the Vice Principal or Principal, or put them in detention. 'Class monitors' (a student elected by the rest of the class) and the class prefect have some disciplinary powers, but these are not defined. You may also throw objects at, but not to hit, the students: for example, stubs of chalk, or wooden blackboard dusters. You should not keep still. Prowl. Range around the class in between the rows, 'picking up' homework by suddenly pointing at someone and demanding an entire conjugation of the imperfect subjunctive of an irregular Spanish verb. If they fail and in gesturing with the yardstick you hit them, that is fair. As a teacher, you must smile often because these are understood to be preparatory games for life, full of enjoyment and energy. Students who finish all the set work and extra sets too easily should be put to help their most difficult peers, rather than allowed to exceed the lesson plans too far. Homework must be presented in an A5 lined copybook dedicated to that subject and with the student's name, class and subject on the front. Exercises must be written in blue or black pen, legibly, in cursive, except for some Maths, Science and Geography assignments, which must be completed in sharp pencil of the grade specified by the teacher, in the designated book (project book, scrap book, graph book, etc.).

GENERATING 'SYNTAX POEMS' FROM CLOSE READING OF 'I AM NO SOLDIER'

SYNTAX POEM VI: CASE STUDY

Joining and skipping

Here the question is is to do with joining (and skipping). Glance quickly down the page. What is the very first word of each stanza? Extract these to make the skeleton turns of a poem. Notice how your eye passes right to left at a line break. What is the smallest unit of sense that arises from the joining-up made by the eye-movement (or that catches the inner ear as the eye moves)? Enjoy this possible naïve transition – how it skitters away from the right margin's space, away from auditory memory. Enjoy this without letting your mind edit and select it out in favour of larger patterns.

The syntax poem might not work as a text *for* performance. It is, however, a performance text, in so far as these skeleton turns become something to think with, when trying out voice and movement, or collecting and creating objects to dress the blackbox space.

Soldered transitions

Transcribing the illegitimate sense made by joining and skipping gives rise to what we felt as 'soldered transitions'. Taking the time to make this transcription of the source's parts, we noticed several features of the poem as a whole. Here are some examples.

In stanza 3, we could not break the short line 'peeping at daylight' into units that would make a transition between the preceding and subsequent lines. Taking our cue from the triple structures into which the poem naturally articulates itself, we began looking for other three-word lines and three-word units. There are so many of these that we experienced them as agglomerations and rhythms. In our readings out loud, 'I Am No Soldier' generally felt long-breathed. So, at this juncture in re-reading for 'syntax poems', the contrast made by the brevity of the three-word lines caught our interest: stanza 2, 'moon of terror'; stanza 3, 'peeping at daylight'; stanza 5, 'I shall arise', 'I shall arise'; stanza 6, 'Come comrade stargazer'.

We felt that the short lines were voluminous. After marking the first line's setting up of a triplet structure with 'Wherever you fall' / 'I shall arise', we breathed space around the three-word single-line units. We thought of the written lines as extending into the dimensions of crowds and galaxies. We thought, too, of the poem as a series of sounds being uttered during and above a procession or protest. We tried to think our way into how the pattern of triple fixtures might help with memorisation for a solitary reader during confinement in a house, or (like Carter) in jail.

Breathing the poem's units for their length, we found that the 'hempen pendulum' line in stanza 4 is both unusually long, and resistant to division. Sometimes its metronomical ticking sounded like dolorous prolongation. Sometimes it measured out the threat of execution.

Taking time over the transitions between lines uncovered, or let us create, other patterns. Using the mouth, tongue and lips, being aware of the soft palate and the back of the throat, in utterance, we experienced the tension and release intrinsic to the poem's physical form as a sound-object designed for replay by human anatomy. Experimenting with the cry or gape of the 'I' and 'O' of the last stanza (of which more soon), we noticed the nearby occurrence of the physically high long vowel /i/ (ee) in 'breed', 'freedom', 'seen', 'seeds', 'wheel', 'dream', which requires stretching and tautening of facial muscles. Similarly, when concentrating on the poem as a visual object, we appreciated better how the last stanza's sense of transformation (revolutionary; shamanistic) arises in part from how its words look like: just a few letters could be transposed to wheel one wordform into another.

Although our 'soldered transitions' approach to producing some of the syntax poems brought up non-sense line breaks, we kept some of these in performance, for a clamour which might evoke the letting fall of identity. We saw these as an intensification of Carter's power to be elliptical, as evidenced by the final verb applying equally to poet, poem and sacrifice.

MORE SYNTAX POEM APPROACHES

Reading for skeletons and patterns brings up how Carter's polemical, memoiristic prose shares numerous techniques and features with his poetry. The sense of time as both potential and historical is intensified by the movement between infinitive and past forms of the same verb to create a ring of consciousness. As mentioned before, Carter favours clear, large tripartite structures.

Threes

While we had the advantage of being able to realise the poem in performance through simultaneous different readings and movements, for example with a call and response approach to unify the fragments of the syntax poems, or playing fragmentation off against 'whole' recitations, we relied on Carter's interlacing triple rhythms and echoes to keep perspective on 'I Am No Soldier'. The text's wide compass of place and time, and the poetic persona's existence and ability to reach through these, play off a triple 'no' as well as assertions.

Our practice did not involve actor-like rehearsal of a finished play script. We preferred singer-like explorations of the poem's nuances and scope. We reinflected, and listened reflectively to, the first stanza, considering how we could move the audience to an awareness of its positioning, from 'Wherever…Wherever…whenever', 'into an arctic night…in particular gladness…In this hopeful dawn of earth'. The second stanza's treble description of Africa in stanza 2, 'unhappy Africa / unhappy lake of sunlight / moon of terror' became the opportunity for an expansion of elemental and geographical scope, voiced in a way to summon the opposite of the alleged unhappiness. The exclamations at the close of the third stanza, 'Cold rain is mist! Is air, is all my breath!' uses the simple 'is' three times to effect a dissolution of boundaries between external and internal weather. This leads up to the fourth stanza's imprisoned speaker. By poetic patterning, he is able to bind a threefold time of suffering into one line ('one minute and one hour and one year'), then to exceed his prison cell: his spiritual/political vision escapes, launching a vast ship on the ocean of life. In stanza five, we activated the triple rhythms to bring restlessness to the controversial claims 'If it is in… If it is in… If it is in…' (displacing the rained 'is') and the invocation of named places (Malaya, Kenya, Korea). After this, the three-times repeated 'I shall arise' strikes more like a prophecy or a certainty, not a mere foreshadowing, of total change or resurrection.

The triple pattern may be a rhetorical commonplace, but with Carter as political preacherman (compare Gerard Manley Hopkins transfusing Heraclitean fire into his Christian self-fashioning) there is a transfusion of the traditional emotional power of the poetics of redemption into his reiterated 'I am' and 'I come'. The explosive dance we improvised at the end of our performance derives from the text's bursting of its own three-pattern into a five (hand, breast, head, dream, blood).

Spiral revolving

The echoing of each other's voices, and our pulling and tugging each other's glittery scarves to stay connected in the dance, drew inspiration from the text's 'revolutionary', circular, or spiralling structure. We traced these from 'Wherever' in the first stanza to 'O wherever' in the seventh (last) stanza. The first stanza builds momentum via a series of disavowals, a list of negations – 'no soldier', 'no hunter of men', 'no human dog of death' – whereas the last stanza uses conjunctions ('and') to build lists of peoples (four 'ands'), cosmic features and the body (three 'ands'). We tried to embody the shift from an atomised 'my', the first person singular possessive pronoun of 'I am my poem' (stanza 1) to the outward-turned signalling of the deictic 'this': 'I am this poem'. As the poetic voice grows to its conclusion and as our dance whirled, so the individual vow 'I come to you' (stanza 1) is surpassed by the great call 'O come astronomer of freedom'.

Inner/outer

With the schoolroom, resurrection yard, wire-fenced compound and galactic dance space co-existent in the blackbox studio, and the audience dispersed, standing, sitting, or moving as they pleased, we had to anchor ourselves in the text and live out its twists and turns, in order to make sure we did not get physically stuck at any random or significant point in the set-that-was-not-a-set.

We took one cue from the turning point in stanza three, signalled in time by 'But now...for a moment' and by the physical location of the speaker in a prison cell. This gives way from stanza two to participial forms: 'emitting', '[s]winging', 'burning', 'pointing'.

These non-finite verbs create a speaker who is charged inwardly with 'tomorrow', a potentiality beyond any location or instant. Stanza three effects a political and poetic magic, as the prison ceiling becomes 'the sky's black paint' and another participial form shows it 'falling into fragments'. In action, we lived this out, not during a reading of stanza three, but much later in the performance: during our reading of the pure syntax poems, when the text's tearing-apart was accompanied by our bodies' falling to the floor or into each other's laps via temporary deaths/spirit possession, then succeeded by the communal ecstasy of dance. We derived this ecstasy not only from the poem's magnificent close, but from its heart, stanza 4 where the speaker-prisoner's inner empowerment, despite literal and figurative bandages and executions, enables him to use the imperative 'go' plus a participial verb of action, in 'Vast ship go sailing'. Once again, we sensed a dimension that exceeded the words: here, a reversal of the traumatic 'Middle Passage' voyages of slave ships, into an ark-like transit that embraces all 'comrades'.

The floating 'of'

Looking to create connexions between ourselves, the audience, Carter's poem and the poem's context and conceptual world, we were sensitive to how the text creates connexions (cf. the joining, skipping and soldered transitions in Syntax Poem VI). We noticed a great many 'of' constructions, where 'of' has a floating value, not always being an indication of origin or possession. These create a natural-feeling series of connexions between minute and vast, abstract and concrete, emotional and cosmic: 'hopeful dawn of earth', 'insurgent geography of my life', 'latitudes of anguish', 'poles of my frozen agonies', 'my regions of grief', 'the burning compass of tomorrow', etc. through to 'sun's acres of children and of mornings', culminating in the last stanza's triple 'of': 'In the whirling cosmos of my soul there are galaxies of happiness... O come astronomer of freedom'.

Overanalyzing the text when making a performance with syntax poems is a risk. In trying out what kinds of joins are made by 'of', we started to discover – but did not pursue too far – the joins made by 'there'. Starting with the idea of location, from the opening stanza's 'Wherever...Wherever and whenever' moving to the next stanza's 'somewhere in blood', which has the horror of being neither unspecific nor specific, we found the poem offering abstract/concrete, individual/cosmic fulfilments in 'there' constructions: 'there will I come' (stanza 1); 'There is a dark island in a dark river' (stanza 3); 'There is a nightmare bandaged on my brow' (stanza 4), a turning point without 'there' but with when/when/wherever/where/where/where (stanza 5); 'there are galaxies of happiness' (stanza 7).

SYNTAX POEM CHARTS

Our working materials towards a performance based on 'I Am No Soldier' included charts such as the following. It is not given as a definitive guide or academic interpretation. Like all the other materials included in this section, this chart is a record of the ephemeral. These materials are primarily an encouragement to readers to prepare their own kinetic, immersive, or collaborative responses (should they so wish) to any text of their choice. The texts in *Skin Can Hold* can be read as poems, but they also have been designed for such treatment.

I, O

There are vowel patterns visible as shapes ('In the insurgent') ('is mist! is air, is all my breath!') suggestive of compression, verticality, inclusion, irruption or compass ('O come astronomer of freedom'). Technically a vowel has no physical 'stop' for the airstream. In 'I Am No Soldier', 'O' is a crucial patterning cry of freedom. In performance, or reading out loud, it also works musically and physically, freeing the breath at the start of a series of words. Sometimes 'O' is a pointer towards the poem's imaginative content. Sometimes it is a vocative; sometimes it raises the poem into a summoning. 'O' is a cry, but a cry is not necessarily outward. The direction of the 'O' can be outward, in common with Martin Carter's universal, compassing poetics. Alternatively, 'O' in physical utterance and/or in emotion can be inward, almost inhaled, implosive, in contrast to its physical production as a vowel sound. Here is how we understood some instances of 'O' in 'I Am No Soldier'.

O comrade unknown to me falling somewhere in blood	stz. 2, l. 1	Individual to generalised individual, reaching out, vocative, calling. Only stz. 2 and the final stanza begin with the 'O' outcry.
O my heart is a magnet / electrified	stz. 2, l. 5	Exclamation, interior, effecting imaginative transformation as the speaker gains force.
O forest of torture	stz. 3, l. 5	Gestures towards (thereby imaginatively creating) an interior geography of the speaker that fuses with the physical geography of Guyana and of the suffering body. Continues pattern of 'O' as a mid-stanza irruption of air, of all the breath.
O current of pain and channel of endurance	stz. 3, l. 6	As above, creating a three-pattern of the interior/exterior fusion.
O life's mapmaker chart me now an ocean	stz. 4, l. 5	Once more five lines in. A direct vocative, effecting a quasi-shamanistic escape from the cell. Visually this echoes whilst opening/undoing the 'o' closed by a negative 'n' sound in the immediately previous line which consists of an executioner's metronome-count of 'one minute and one hour and one year' over 'bloody dust'. It also introduces the free flow and spattering of saliva if the sound 'O' is physically articulated, redeeming the 'bloody dust'.
O wherever you fall comrade I shall arise.	stz. 7, l. 1	This direct vocative 'O' is stanza-initial for just the second time in the poem, rephrasing the other stanza-initial call to 'O comrade unknown to me'. The poetic voice has attained an assurance of promise and reach, connecting with any and every comrade through and beyond change and calamity – comradely love stronger than death.
O come astronomer of freedom / Come comrade stargazer	stz. 7, l. 6	This final call gains power not only from its phonetic shape and semantic content, but because it fulfils the musical expectation set up for the 'O' cry to occur at initial and/or medial (c. line 5 or 6) points in stanzas. At a semantic level, it fuses the appeal to any individual comrade with the appeal to those imaginary or imaginative figures like 'life's mapmaker' who exercise a wide and strange power to bring about real change.

V
IN FLAMES

FIELD POSTCARD: RONDEAU-STYLE TEXT

Nothing is to be written on this side
except the date and signature of the sender.
Sentences not required may be erased.
If anything else is added the postcard will be destroyed.

So carry marigolds, show sorrow: hide
July war in flowers at home; their code is tender.
Nothing is to be written on this side
except the date and signature of the sender.

April he fell in flames; lilies of the valley implied
humility, poppies oblivion; tender
your papers – no letter lately wounded, no parcel well erased,
apple blossom admitted, rose follows, iris destroyed.

Nothing is to be written on this side
except the date and signature of the sender.
Sentences not required may be erased.
If anything else is added the postcard will be destroyed.

Pillars of fire terror like Money for ever
Strange ghosts emptiness and drink whispered
Fire laughing glistening
Ardent wires listening
Strange joy underground engines
Dance of Death still the divider ritual incising
Death was young sacrifice a bullet sang
Strange arithmetic life without livelong
Death fell through twisting galleries
Who fired dreams agony
Strangely illumined brains spattered red
Game with Death green fields

Tidings / none know which / screaming
Loves came out / Hector and Lysander / singing
Millions and millions / blindfold / banging a gong
Shells go crying / returning / more sound
Blossoming / silhouettes / grant us
God / joy and blindness / the Face
Miles and miles / damned / pious poetry
This hid riot / endure / quietly
Oh, you were / my own / a Heart crying
Be animal / crawling grass / to our dying
is mine / was mine / a cadency
like a flood / exquisite like limbs / senselessly
play / without the war / continued; pain
there is / oh! / none to proclaim
clay / only yesterday / recalling singing

Ha Mort, le port commun

SOURCES: Guillaume de Machaut,'Hareu! hareu! le feu, le feu; Helas! où sera pris confors; Obediens usque ad mortem' (M10). Pierre de Ronsard, 'Ah longues nuicts d'hyver', in *Derniers vers*. Tim Kendall (ed.), *Poetry of the First World War* (OUP, 2013).

THIS IS YOUR HOME (YOU HAVE NO OTHER)

Are you the person
who goes around taking off
all the lights
Are you the person
Are you the person
who insists on asking things
about food
Are you the person
Are you the person
who made us forget about fast day
and drink shots
Are you the person
Are you the person
we'd listen to if your voice
wasn't rough
Are you the person
Are you the person
with no friends no friends except
those people
Are you the person
Are you the person
who'll only go out somewhere
difficult
Are you the person
Are you the person
who ought to do mythical
magical
tricks so this poem
can end with a blast
welcome home

SINCERE

from *Etymology for British Voters*

lit up with it:
sincere: sin wax
hot strips applied
rip out: without
wax or harvest:
sincere: counting
prived of zeroes:
since when since year
zero: limits
drip and take form:
face it: sincere:
pareidolia
scalding water-
fall: as if sinc-
is compounding
saxon before
this time rings break
for giving out:
he who gives out
must be in charge:
sincere: not these
romance roots: clean
unlike a lung

SNOWGLOBE

Fear: mild to moderate at ground level
unnoticeable in coastal regions
disappearing quickly at altitude.

How are you feeling?

Geological.
The sky is the limit.

Tell us about those
wisps, dorothying, azraelling, powered
by nothing reporters could brighten
a trail out of...?

The special equipment,
language, commonly accused of failure,
thrown like rope. Here.
Rounding the corner,
a chaos of crossroads, chicken wire,
the lifting of deep earth.

Why don't you use
a gift like that? Everyone's digging for poems.

So when did you decide you were afraid?

I did not.
I did not say good morning,
look up or down or left or right, or think
of sex of age of colour.

I began to count

the line of hi-vis men sitting
starlings and chaffinches on a wire
entirely birdlike
at ankle height
or half as much again above the house.

Then there were more
stiltwalking
as birds do
still not men, except their speech
Polish and Irish voices:

With each phrase they curve

the sky contracting

two feet untunnelled
mind almost flashed back to human names
such voices once meant me by naming,
kindly.

With each phrase eye-light came on.

Went out.

Void

in between.

The birds have flown for counting.
Because the fear has been allayed.
It was
in having gone.

Because the brilliancy
also is gone.
Being scaled to matter.

Because the day's flagged-up appointment stood.
Six rainbow vials to be filled with blood.

FRAGMENT OF A LOST EPIC FROM THE LOSING SIDE

What is the insomnia of insomnia?
Where is the bleached anguish of the night?
The city listened.
The army waited in the streets.
The young men waited to pour into the streets.
The young women waited indoors.

The dust whispered and skittered under the feet
that audibly tried to make no noise.
The city waited
The army was on the move
The women listened from within the darkened windows
The city would never be so bright again.

A shape like crossed forearms held up to shelter the face
appeared in the metal of the sky
...

...   and he is stricken.
He is stricken as men who are stricken are stricken.
The youngest keyholder of the city. My child.
I write this kneeling on a stone bridge, unsupported,
so high above the street that the mists mingle under
with time to burn off
and as if river were the running in the streets
and the mist from fighting were the mist from water
...

NOTE: The rest of the translation has not been recovered

108

INTERVENTIONS AROUND A CITY

This ritual is not intended to cleanse
This ritual is to wash away the ritual

The removal of the roofs is intended
to restore a sense of the original roofs

The grandeur of the buildings which were wiped out
may be reconceivable by the sky's grandeur

To return it to sand how can you say that
(of course you didn't) when it was not raised from sand

To repair it with open water courses
where was water's deeper hiding place from burning air

To plant it with orchards how can you plan that
(what grows) a foreign-owned desalination plant

The veins of this earth are baked with alphabets.
View strikes as vascular surgery on plaqued earth.

POEMS FOR THE DOUMA 4

With thanks to English PEN and Steven Fowler. For Razan Zaitouneh, Samira Al-Khalil, Wa'el Hamada and Nazim Hammadi, abducted in December 2012 from their workplace, the Violations Documentation Centre, Syria

I

Eyes are weeping in the face;
in the same face, the mouth is speaking.
The uncoupling of tears from speech
in those who offer witness
in words; whose bodies, blue
or red from beating, were dancing
where dancing meets shooting;
singing, where silence wants
just one sentence.

Just one sentence.

How does that make you feel?

That one whose fluency in words
has come uncoupled from the fluids
tracking the face during talking
rolling out truthful paragraphs
while souls blister out from ducts,
stops. Tears and speech
together. Stopped by *feelings*.
The answer is only in the eyelids.
The language has arms of our supplying.

II

The facility of lists:
unarmed – unknown – masked –
betrayal – won't forget – won't ignore –
Nuance has more off switches than lovers.
Men stormed.
Men do not storm.
These are not natural phenomena.
Sometimes I hate my trained mind.

III

What a thing it is to lift the photos, pictures, placards and posters
of people who were, should be, might be, are alive. What a process.
What it is to process through the streets, not standing shoulder
to shoulder with, not seen as standing on the shoulders of, those
heroically beloved and otherwise who have gone before this and ten
thousand years before, but to share the process of lifting aloft the
image of them in two dimensions. All this being the condition in
which to gift them body and time.

What a possibility of making *nice local people* angry, alienating
potential allies, losing actual neighbours, by bearing aloft, as
Birnam Wood to Dunsinane, an army of martyr-faces like new and
unkillable migrants; strange fruit that ghost the Sunday table. What
a possibility of making a mirror of mourning in which the brown
dead bud out in too many particulars: chess champions, party
girls, lawyers and gardeners. What a possible shame and fear and
revulsion: don't make them like *us*, don't bring them too close, don't
claim they are like *us*; they are unimaginable, and keep them so,
for we already find this little island hard to live on, and identity is
mortality, must remain unimaginable, must leave *us* cold.

IV

The facility of lists.
After seeing footage
from the detention centre,
I wanted to ban
mannequins, bar
codes, and loaves
of sliced bread.

VI
EPILOGUE

RINGING VÖLUNDARKVIÐA / WAYLAND SMITH MOVES

For two bodies and a live or recorded chorus.

I. SWANMAIDEN

From the south.
To the coast.
Are you tuning into fortune?

Towards forest.
To rest.
What fate is playing you?

Check on the weather
for hunting.

Chase down the weather
for turning.

Come in and go out and look about.
Go out and come in and look about.

Enemies would nail you and scrape the moon pale.

Whatever you have,
enemies would take it.
Whatever you seek,
enemies would take it.
Take.
Take.
Take.

Whatever you love,
enemies would drop it.
Whatever you make,
enemies would drop it.
Drop.
Drop.

Love, sleep in expectation.
O love, waken in dejection.

Your hands that worked metal are weighted with metal.
Your feet are fettered; your tendons are scissored.

They legislate that they have taken what you owe them.
You lament that they have taken what you own.

O my river of swansdown.
O my heart of gold.

II. HUNTERS AND GOVERNMENT

We like what he does.
We like it so much
we'll send to the forest
and have him trussed up,
indentured, and hamstrung:
the workmanlike guest
of a wealthy host.
Let him have an island
which he must not leave;
exercise his traditions,
since he cannot leave.

III. ARTISANAL, ISOLATE

I am the guest you keep
because you can use, have used,
or cannot avoid them;
yet your surprise
when I lure your sons to their death
is endless;
when I silver their skulls
and return them for you to drink from,
when by smithcraft I prise out their eyes
and reset them as bling
for your sacrosanct, ignorant women.

I am the prisoner
whose wife allegedly had flown away.
I who had joy am joyless
and make joylessness
and fool your daughter
and fill her with grandchildren
and stamp out your laughter.
Though I languish under your vigilance,
my wounds are wings.
Watch me go,
if you can see how
my love and I never stopped flying.

ACKNOWLEDGEMENTS

This book owes its core section to the generosity of Neil Astley, who has permitted the reproduction of Martin Carter's 'I Am No Soldier' from Martin Carter, *University of Hunger: Collected Poems and Selected Prose*, ed. by Gemma Robinson (Bloodaxe, 2006).

Thanks to: Leila Capildeo; Kat Addis and Joseph Minden; Andre Bagoo; Belmont Exotic Stylish Sailors; Tessa Berring; the British Council; Dave Coates; Sasha Dugdale and family; Ian Duhig; Suzannah V. Evans; SJ Fowler; K.M. Grant and family; Curtis Gross; Selina Guinness, Colin Graham and family; Bowie Guinness-Graham; Lucy Hannah; Susannah Herbert and family; Fedon Honoré; Alex Houen; Dimitra Ioannou; Peadar King and Inishbofin crew; Maria Jastrzębska and Deborah Price; Nicholas Laughlin; Gail McConnell; Rob Mackenzie; Ron Paste; Marina Salandy Brown; Rosie Šnajdr; Johnny Stollmeyer; J.R. Thorpe and Dai Bowe; the Tods of Norfolk; John Whale; Lydia Wilson.

Especial thanks to Douglas Caster and the University of Leeds, where the Douglas Caster Cultural Fellowship in Poetry (2017–19) allowed this book to be completed. Equal thanks to the University of Cambridge (and Murray Edwards College) for the Judith E. Wilson Fellowship in Poetry (2014–15), and to fellow theatre-makers 2014–16, including Jo Cobb, Hope Doherty, Jeremy Hardingham, Fern Richards, Olivia Scott-Berry and Paige Smeaton.

Work has appeared in, been performed at, or commissioned by: *aglimpseof* https://aglimpseof.net/; *Cambridge Literary Review*; *The Compass Magazine* (www.thecompassmagazine.co.uk); *The Irish Review*; *Spark: Poetry and Art Inspired by the Novels of Muriel Spark*, ed. by Rob Mackenzie and Louise Peterkin (Blue Diode Press, 2018); The Bocas Litfest; Sophie Collins, for the Glasgow Women's Library; English PEN; INISH: Island Conversations; National Poetry Day; The National Poetry Library, Southbank Centre; the Scottish Poetry Library.

Any omissions or oversights are my own.